ALSO PUBLISH

MW01267889

Library of Congress Cataloguing in Publication Data

I Know Who You Are, But What Am I / Ali Sands

ISBN: 978-0-9860844-7-8

Transgress Press, Oakland, California

I Know Who You Are,
But What Am I?

I Know Who You Are, But What Am I?

A Partner's Perspective on Transgender Love

Ali Sands

For her and for him
and
for who we've become

Taken out of context, I must seem so strange

-Ani Difranco

Acknowledgements

With immense gratitude to the Trans/Queer community of Minneapolis: Thank you for holding the net every time we jumped off. I see you and you will be our family forever. To the community members of Wellfleet for bringing us into the fold and loving us for who we are. To Marianne Barnett and Shari Ballard, brilliant friends who lifted up this project in ways others cannot. Thanks to Amy Voll for your amazing creative talent on the book cover. Julie, thank you for every word and every tear you have shed with your badass acceptance and validating love. To Marya who I have never had to explain one minute of this journey to…parallel lives, girl. For giving me the validating and accepting love that got me here, thank you, Chelsea and Eli. You are my heart. To Rhys, the truest person I have ever known, for sharing this depth and intimacy with me and letting me find myself through your vulnerability…Ungowa, baby. To my publisher, Trystan Cotten, who became an editor, mentor and friend: I appreciate you.

I KNOW WHO YOU ARE,
BUT WHAT AM I?

Contents

Preface

CHANGE. Such an insidious and often painful companion. Change has delivered me sorrow and loss, yet so much knowledge. I will never regret its unrelenting companionship. Recent experiences of my life—at once, compelling and propelling—have been magnified and made invaluable by change.

Five years ago, I was a 38 year-old woman living in the suburbs with my husband of twenty years. We had been "high-school sweet-hearts" but regretfully we never evaluated our relationship beyond that. Somewhere along the way our marriage became an increasingly platonic one. I knew my responsibilities, he knew his. My greatest asset and most deeply ingrained coping mechanism was painting a picture of perfection for everyone around me and, even more dangerously, for myself. I was a master at creating every little nuance necessary to make sure the rest of the world saw my life as perfect. I had two beautiful children—the constant joys of my existence—who were always dressed in my latest creations as a seamstress, a husband with multiple college degrees who earned an adequate income, as well as the presence and support of our extended families who were ever present in our daily lives. We traveled, celebrated birthdays, and entertained friends on a regular basis.

One year became five, and ten grew into twenty. Our house was always clean, inviting, and we had an "open-door-policy" to numerous friends and family. Many of those friends were lesbians.

Were those friendships early signs of my general discontent with my suburban heterosexual lifestyle? In truth, I often sought out the companionship of lesbian identified women. Not easy to do in the conservative northern suburbs of the Twin Cities area. However, since I had grown up in a very liberal environment, I thought nothing of these strong attachments to women who loved other women. After all, I considered myself to be an open-minded individual who valued diversity. Besides, my marriage was perfect, *right?* And of course I had no plans of *ever* leaving the fabricated security of the little utopia I had so carefully constructed.

At that time, I lived less than two miles from my mother, who began most of her sentences with "me" or "I." My father died an untimely death when I was just 21. The impact of his alcoholism and perhaps unexpected unconditional love had already been imprinted on me. I remained enmeshed and steeped in family dysfunction so thick that cloaked as I was in its numbing patterns, I could see little of my authentic self. Only with physical distance and years of therapy was I able to begin to excavate a truth uniquely my own.

Discontent was my constant, yet unwelcomed, ally. It revealed itself in so many ways: the repeated, sometimes obsessive, rearranging of furniture, even to the extreme of maneuvering a grand piano across the living room by myself. My (then) husband would come home from work and exclaim, "How the *hell* did you manage *that?!*" I had a lot of friends who I encouraged to stay close by and was a constant caregiver to all of them. But the most important ingredient in my recipe of discontent was my immense dissatisfaction and ongoing preoccupation with my physical appearance. The latter was the easiest to rationalize, considering I lived and held community in upper middle-class suburbia. I valiantly attempted to "fit in" with all the other kids' moms. But all the makeup in Target couldn't paint a pretty face over my impending sense of emptiness. Eventually my nose ring and tattoo emerged as bold statements of my independence. Upon nearing my 40th birthday I had two amazing teenagers, one about to launch into college, and a husband from whom I was so emotionally detached that many of my "friendships" (male *and* female), had become spirited emotional affairs. In addition, I experienced a gnawing feeling within my body that slowly began to manifest as physical illness. All of these superbly crafted distractions were the fortress that protected my wounded soul.

My entire existence for the past thirty years had balanced on my innate aptitude at maintaining one disgusting little secret. For a brief period of three years, from age 9 to 12, which felt as though it lasted all of eternity, my maternal grandfather sexually molested and psychologically tormented me in my own home. He was brought in and presented as "family" by the people I trusted most—my parents. It was no wonder then, that when he began his powerful and perverse little games, I learned quickly and with conviction to keep my nine-year-old mouth shut. There was no room for blatant honesty in my household. This was our family's tacit rule. The only reason there was an end to my abuse was that the end came of him. I was somehow able to maintain a level of control through external focus. Ah, yes, it turned out that being adept at managing and soothing everyone else's problems only gave me more momentum to run from my own. I had sprinted full force into the wall of codependency.

Here was the point where the running stopped. I spoke the words aloud... *I was sexually abused.*

My life exploded and the pattern of perfection I had so carefully constructed was in tiny pieces. It was during this time in my life that Dr. T. swaggered into the room—literally. Having been with my husband since I was 17, I was naive about matters of the heart. I had no idea that what I was feeling could have been anything other than a strong fondness. All I knew at the time was that I wanted more than anything to be near *her*. When we met, she was also in a committed yet dysfunctional marriage. It was not much different from my own, save one minor detail; her's was a lesbian marriage. I felt nothing immoral about our connection. I was very "above board" with my husband, openly spilling my guts about my awesome new friendship. This honesty and vulnerability would later become the undoing of our marriage. I reasoned that Dr. T. was female, as was I, and there could be no harm in that, since I was after all, not a lesbian, but a straight woman, married with two children and living in suburban America. I knew my role.

Masculinity was her essence. The way she sat: feet planted firmly on the ground, knees apart, allowing room for whatever was at the meeting place of her thighs. She opened doors for me and positioned herself between me and anyone she perceived to be a threat. Her hair was a silvery salt-and-pepper, cut in a crew, and impeccably groomed.

Masculine clothing was the only attire she ever wore, and leather boots were always on her feet.

She drove a truck and liked to smoke an occasional, good cigar. When she did, the sight of it brought me to my knees. She had the faintest air of expensive men's cologne, and she loved women for being the mystery we often are. Our friendship forced me to look at who I really was. She allowed me, without even knowing it, to begin to see myself the way she saw me…as a woman. I can honestly say now that I didn't know if I was in the relationship because of how much I liked her, or because of how much I began to like myself when she was near. All I knew was that I wanted to know more about this remarkable person who had been hiding inside—the "me" that was *woman*.

Growing up poor in New Jersey with eleven siblings, only one a brother,—had taught her nothing of the masculinity she presented in her daily life. As a matter of fact, she vividly recalls one of her more persistent sisters trying desperately (and to no avail) to instruct her on how to act like a girl, "pull your arms in by your sides," "don't stand with your legs so far apart!"

Growing up, Dr. T. was a typical tomboy of the seventies. Irish/Italian, Catholic; she knew nothing except the binary gender roles (male/female) that most of us are presented with in our youth. And yet she always had a sense that she did not fit in the gender binary. The one saving grace in this growing incongruity of self was her mother. Her mom had the amazing ability of balancing an unconditional love with a level of indifference to her child's eccentricities. As a child, Dr. T. was allowed to climb trees, play sports, and wear Tough Skins jeans every day. For the most part, her daily existence wasn't impeded by the gender biases of the 1970s. However, even with this tremendous maternal love and acceptance, she grew into an adult with an enormous chip on her shoulder. She was angry and wanted the world to know it at every chance, even if she was clueless about where that anger came from.

She spoke of feeling "incongruent," even at the age of five or six. It was her dream at that young age to grow up and get married: to be a strong, providing husband for a beautiful wife. When puberty hit, she was dismayed to discover the cultural expectation that *she* would be the wife married to a man. She avoided the convent (unlike a few of her sisters) as a way out of her family home, and college became her respite. There, her attraction to women only grew, constantly confirmed by a new population of women in her life—LESBIANS! Ironic, then, since the day I met Dr. T. she adamantly and with conviction stood on the belief that she is most certainly *not* a lesbian! She defied everything about the lesbian culture in which she surprisingly found herself.

I found myself listening to a litany of gender injustices every time she spoke. Dr. T. knew the day she was coldly informed by her parents that she could no longer venture around the neighborhood without a shirt, that there was a great discrepancy between her mind, her body and her beautiful, resilient spirit.

I knew as well. Our relationship was different than that between two females. I felt her masculinity and became the femme I was. I allowed her to do things for me that I had never in all of my history allowed anyone else to do: open doors, pay for dinner, and carry anything she deemed "too heavy" for me. She began slowly...very slowly, to trust me. My marriage was quickly unraveling, and I shared these feelings with her. In my vulnerability, I found validation for the first time in my entire life. I didn't know it at the time, but in those moments we were building an unspoken trust. A trust that was very important.

Often in my life during times of chaos, I have initiated some of the most important lasting relationships of my life.

Chaos...

When I speak the word, the feelings that I connect to are all the remnants of my marriage coming to its physical end. I do mean physical, because emotionally it had been ending for a very long time.

As T. and I grew closer and more trusting of one another, I came to love her. I fell in love in a way I never thought possible. Our childish vulnerability with one another allowed Dr. T. a window into her own opening soul. And what she saw there she could no longer ignore...a man. Change became my guiding beacon.

∼

I put pen to paper the first time that T. told me s/he thought that s/he was transgender. Initially, a journal for my own benefit, my daily musings became a passionate connection in our relationship. I would frequently read aloud to T. what I had written. Three years of transitioning have since passed, and throughout I continued my strong commitment to journaling the experiences of being in love with a transitioning, transgender, man.

There were times I realized *my* transition to be *as* dramatic and difficult as his. Along this journey it was difficult to find both support and basic information. I needed to navigate his transition and remain emotionally intact. I quickly found that very little had been written about the partners of transgender people. After my own long journey, I realize that the rawness of this experience is worthy of its own voice—its own story. And raw it is.

I am immensely grateful to Rhys for allowing me to share our intimate story. I believe leaving each entry in its original voice casts a light on the pain and the beauty through which our relationship has persevered and continues to thrive today. It is my hope that my honest writing will open conversations which bring greater understanding and healing to the reader.

CHAPTER 1
The Epiphany

February 2005

I'VE BEEN IN AN INTIMATE RELATIONSHIP with a female-bodied person for a few years now. She, however, does not identify as a female, and she is definitely not a woman. What we have between us is profoundly, emotionally intimate. My vulnerability with her, I didn't think to be possible. We don't exactly identify as a lesbian couple, and yet we have found no other label that accurately describes us. In addition, the lesbian community is the only place she has ever had a social network. She is the man and I the woman in a relationship that is ironically, very traditionally heterosexual. She is incredibly masculine and has worn only male clothing since early childhood. With her ten sisters incapable of fulfilling T.'s need for a male role model, her mom let her shop in the boys' department at Sears, even in the 1970s. Amazing! She has known and believed since she was three years old, that she is a boy. She thought as a child that as she grew, her body would change accordingly to match her innate sense of her own male identity. She was waiting for a penis. As the teenage years approached, T. was forced to wear a shirt to cover the budding little lies that were becoming her own body—female breasts. Yet, her body and mind weren't travelling on the same road. So when my love

1

came to me tonight, pouring out her truth in all its primal rawness, I could find nothing but immense love within myself for her.

T. told me that a close friend asked to interview her for a master's class she is currently taking. When they got together, many questions were asked about T.'s sexual orientation and her gender identity. This was the first time T. was made aware of a possible difference between the two. As the interview continued, the woman finally asked T.: "So if you don't identify as a woman, and you don't know if you are a man, then do you identify as transgender?"

This is where the door of mystery was split wide open for T. She was given a few books on the subject by her friend, and went directly home to read them, cover to cover. Every single word was an unveiling of self. Every story was a connection, a kinship, linking T. to the experiences on the page. T. had never heard of the term "transgender" in all of her 39 years, and yet had lived her entire life in a female body presenting as male. Transgender is an umbrella term for people whose gender identity, expression or behavior is different from those typically associated with their assigned sex at birth. For many, the word transgender is greatly misunderstood. The irony of how a transgender man can live presenting as masculine for nearly forty years without understanding the very basis of his being is astonishing to me. Yet, it is only since T's revelation, that most people have become increasingly aware of the transgender issue in mainstream culture.

April 2005

A decision has been made. T. has christened himself with a new name. A male name, rooted in the Welsh tradition: Rhys. A name that exudes strength and masculinity. As he announced this to me, he sighed, "Where do I go from here?" The thought of all that is required to legally change your name is overwhelming. Now, imagine adding to that, the staggering amount of explaining required to accomplish this in conjunction with reclaiming your gender and changing your biological sex?

I suggested that we contact the Human Rights Campaign as a place to start. I sense Rhys' commitment to whatever lies ahead, and I intend to gently cradle his heart through it all. Daunting as it may seem, Rhys has decided his first step requires sitting down individually with each and every client he currently works with in his small business. He plans to explain in as minimal terms as possible, the process of his transition. He expects many questions, but will answer very few, and none at all specific to the surgeries he chooses. There is great vulnerability in his being so forthcoming with his self-discovery. My guess is that most will not be surprised, but at the same time, the responses could run the gamut from support to disdain. So, as he works on the best words to use to explain his current situation and the impending changes, I am working on my strength and belief that we will make it through this piece without much personal injury. This process has already begun to make an impact on his business practice, as he maneuvers his days in the land of the "gender-changing."

May 2005

Tonight, you told me that you are sure. Absolutely positive. "No going back from here," those were your exact words on the phone. Your voice confirming 41 years of your search for this very moment…for these very words. I am excited and curious and afraid. I fear your pain…and my own response to it. You are so very courageous; I am so protective. Will I allow the medical community to hold your precious body in their hands? This is what I am here for. This depth of love. This understanding. We are truly together in this; I feel it in my core.

June 2005

In the beginning of September my daughter will be marrying. Bravely, Rhys has agreed to come with me. I have no contact with my family of origin, nor would I choose to at any time in the near future. But isn't it ironic how life can sometimes decide these fateful meetings for you? Of course I would be present to support my child, but the child in me wants to run like hell at the mere thought of this gathering.

Allow me to introduce the cast of characters:

My Daughter: Beautiful, smart and talented, she is still reeling

3

from the pain of her parents' divorce, and marrying at the tender age of 20. She is joy.

My Future Son-in-Law: Good term for it, since his maturity level is that of a boy. Exhibits more addictive behaviors than a mother whose daughter is marrying him would like to see.

My Son: A somewhat typical 17-year-old, with hair over his eyes and a curve in his smile perhaps indicating he has just participated in something I might not want to know about. I adore him.

My Ex-Mother and Father-in-law: A traditional 1950s couple, whom I accepted as family for 22 years. They loved me—perhaps they still do—and were greatly confused by my departure.

My "Mother": A spot-on narcissist. Supportive of my ex-husband and apparently unaware of the impact it has on my healing. My mom has a bizarre loyalty to men. All men. We have not spoken in over a year.

Ex-Sister-in-Laws: Three women, two of whom became my close friends. One of those is a fundamentalist Christian and Republican with an open mind. The other has been like my sister and best friend since I was 17.

My Brother and Sister: Our relationships as siblings has from early on, had an unhealthy, adult children-of-an-alcoholic disconnect. They still do.

Extended Family of the Ex: Largely believe that I am completely off my rocker. Since I am no longer married to my ex-husband, I have lost all credibility with them.

My Ex-Husband: Continues to appear clueless as to why I really needed to leave our relationship. Knits his brow in angst whenever he looks at me. Will most likely be accompanied by his new companion and her two young children.

The Minister: My former boss, a Baptist Minister, and a kind man with the same exact name as my deceased father!

Rhys: Pre-op transgender man, the love of my life. Will be the only "out" member of the LGBTQ community present, besides myself.

ME: Mother of the bride, planner of the event, nemesis to the guest list majority. Queer.

I feel like I need a prescription to continue. Rhys and I will be entering into this scene as a couple for the first time. We will be perceived as a gay couple by a group of Christian homophobes. The others are merely pissed at me for leaving the enmeshed family unit. To my knowledge, no one attending that day, besides my two children, understands the term "transgender." I doubt they have ever even heard of it. So from what I understand, their version of my story goes something like this: *I met this bad news butchy girl (T.), told everyone that I was abused as a child, lost a lot of weight, and became a lesbian due to Rhys' powerful influence over me. Then I left my marriage.* I am horrified at the myriad of scenarios that could be played out on this encroaching day.

The reception is being held in the backyard of my dear friends, so there's one up for me. It will only last a couple of hours. Okay, there's another plus. The kids will be there supporting Rhys and me. I guess we will be okay.

We have planned a vacation to Vancouver Island, leaving the morning following my daughter's big day. This alone gets me past the actual event. There will be a future; I need to remind myself daily. The odds seem so stacked against us, I truly marvel at Rhys' boldness in agreeing to go. He said he is doing this for me, which is weird because *I'm* not doing this for me! If this wedding were not for one of my children, I'd already *be* on Vancouver Island!

Lately, a day doesn't pass without conversation between Rhys and me about how we will navigate this looming celebration. Together, we are laying down very specific boundaries: what we are and aren't capable of at the event. Seriously, to some of the other guests we might as well be painted fuchsia. But this is one hot-pink Mama who is going to walk through that day with her head held high and her hand firmly placed in Rhys'. I can see no other way.

July 14 2005

Recently, I received a piece of mail that was unmistakably penned in my mother's handwriting. Rhys and I have a pact: I will not open any mail from my mom until he is physically there to support me. This rule is born of experience. My mother's correspondence as of late has been less than uplifting. So, covered with my emotional armor, I sat across the table from Rhys and read the letter. It was her attempt at "burying the hatchet" in order to create comfort for herself at my daughter's upcoming wedding. She wrote something along the lines of: "We probably can't fix everything, but you owe it to your daughter to make her day as pleasant as possible."

Ah yes, those old familiar feelings, the constant companions of my childhood. Allow me to introduce you to: Guilt and Shame. Guilt and Shame are my mother's most proficient parenting tools. So no wonder she would send them to me all wrapped up in pretty stationery six weeks prior to the nuptials of my child. Guilt and Shame were ardent motivators for the first 38 years of my life. So, quite naturally she would have reason to believe that they would stir me to action. Honestly, her letter made me irate. I had planned this wedding singlehandedly with my daughter and her fiancé, and with the constant love and unfailing support given by Rhys. Then in walks my unsupportive mother with her twisted take on how I should behave. I blew steam for about a day and a half, and then penned my own missive:

Mom,

I have no difficulty being gracious and appropriate in social situations. The upcoming wedding will be no different. As I have supported my daughter in planning her wedding day, and also supported her every day prior, so will I continue to give her that same support throughout her life. I am not in a position to rectify our relationship in order to increase your comfort level.

That's pretty much all I gave her. Being in a socially hostile environment as an out queer person with my transgender boyfriend is reason enough to stay focused on what really matters here. I can risk no distractions at this point. I have been trying to visualize that moment when Rhys and I arrive at the church (!), and ALL eyes turn to us. Oh yes, make no mistake about it, we will be worthy of a stare: Rhys in his black dress pants, Cole Han shoes and impeccably ironed shirt; me in a simple body-hugging black shift with black gloves up to my elbows...we will definitely turn a few fashion challenged suburban heads. Realistically though, the stares won't be focused on fashion, but gender presentation. The last thing I intend to do that day is take care of my mother's emotional needs. The first thing I intend to do is ensure the personal safety of Rhys and myself. There are too many variables to count in this one gathering, and I don't plan on gambling with any one of them. We will simply be there in support of my children and do it in as respectful a manner as possible, depending on what each moment brings.

That said, I am scared shitless.

There's got to be a morning after, I'm here to prove it. We survived the wedding with no more than two hours of constant stares, handshakes with Rhys that barely made skin contact and a mother (yep, that would be mine!) having an emotional breakdown at the sight of me. We are unscathed and empowered by our newfound abilities as a transgender couple facing the world of the binary. I can't help but be future focused. Where will this transition lead us next? Will we be safe? Will there be others?

August 22, 2005

Disappointingly, Rhys has lost about forty percent of his client base in his chiropractic practice to this point after coming out as a transgender man. Do I blame them?

No.

Yes!

No. Of course I want to, but no. People are reactive and when there's misunderstanding, the easiest and safest way out is by retreating. But the mere fact that I know this requires me to write it down, in the hope that others will be educated through my experience. Surprisingly, most of Rhys' previous lesbian friends and patients have been some of the least understanding. It's as though he has committed an act of great betrayal with his proclamation of maleness. I suppose that the irony is he never would have had those friends if he had been openly male identified from the beginning. So now there is a silent shift taking place. We, as a couple, are finding ourselves becoming increasingly isolated in the LGBTQ "community." Even a few of my own heteronormative friends have grown very uncomfortable as I have become more verbal about my relationship with Rhys.

"At least this means you're not a *lesbian*," was one comment spoken with great relief by my close friend of 20 years upon learning of Rhys' transition. *Not a lesbian*? I guess what she believes is that my sexual identity is determined by the person I love (or am having sex with), at any given time.

What really amazes me is how the "straight" couples are beginning to include us in their social circles. Places that were previously off limits for us. There appears to be a silent scrutiny of our relationship occurring on every level. I have these wild imaginings that we are the topic of the day. But what I know for sure, is that something or someone much more interesting will come along tomorrow and grant us reprieve from our current headliner position—our personal fifteen minutes of fame. I also believe that the biggest reason for all of this new fascination is just basic misunderstanding. Yet, in spite of all these reactions the determination in my lover remains; he has waited this long and no one can deny him his freedom of expression. His greatest issue now is the struggle to be recognized as male, even though he has not yet really begun the physical transition.

November 22, 2005

Today marks the medical beginning, Rhys had an appointment with an OB/GYN doctor—how ironic!—to get the permission and prescription for testosterone. We can call her our gatekeeper at this point. We must go through her required protocol for Rhys to make the physical transition. Just one of many.

Together we were lead to a room that was a typical gynecologist's office, painted in soft, feminine pastel pink, with posters of the stages of a fetus during pregnancy, the best reasons to breastfeed your baby, and hotline numbers for women who are victims of domestic violence. As much of the impertinent information you could possibly begin to imagine for a transgender man. This is just where the insidious deletion of the trans population begins. I asked the nurse about the room we were placed in and its blatant inappropriate theme for our visit. Apparently, the clinic is opening a special area for the transgender clients in January. Well, that will be a Happy New Year to us!

As Rhys feared, he was required to have a pelvic exam in order to be allowed consideration for testosterone therapy. I can't begin to describe the humiliation for him in this situation. Perhaps to compare, you could go find the nearest cis-gendered (born in a body congruent with gender identity) male, a real "guy's guy," and ask him how excited he would be about placing his bare feet in the oven mitt covered stirrups of a gynie table to undergo a pelvic exam? Giddyup, cowboy! Nonetheless, this is just one of the many medical procedures required for Rhys to become physically the man he has always identified as. I left the room to give him privacy, and shortly thereafter we left the office together with a prescription for a vial of testosterone. He shared next to nothing about his experience. Once in the car, tears that I had been willing away found their own route and poured down my cheeks.

Rhys was so worried, "What's wrong sweetie, are you okay?" I tried to find the words to describe the immense love that I felt for him in that very moment. This transformation, however difficult, is the most incredible gift of self-love I have ever personally witnessed. I felt so much joy that Rhys has the freedom to finally have peace with himself.

We immediately drove to the pharmacy to get the prescription filled. After a ten-minute wait and a check for $108 Rhys walked out with a brown glass vial, 2" tall, filled with enough testosterone to last four months, and to catapult him into "roid-rage" if not taken as prescribed. The doctor explained that if testosterone is administered into the body too quickly, it can cause increases in anger and other mood swings. To avoid this, the dose is slowly increased over a period of months and, when monitored with regular lab tests, the change in rage level should be minimal. Damn good thing too, considering that my Jersey-born-and-raised trans man who I so dearly love, is already inclined to "east-coast outbursts" at any given moment. "Not-for-nothin' but," is a common phrase in his vocabulary, which is a Jersey warning sentence that something mean is coming next.

Returning back to Rhys' house, we sat down together with a book written by Loren Cameron, *Body Alchemy*. It is to date the most respectful collection of photographs and biographies depicting trans men before and after their transitions. There was so much excitement between us for the potential of Rhys' body transformation, we were downright giddy! I mean this guy, Loren Cameron, he is absolutely ripped! It's encouraging to any transitioning trans man to know that he has the potential to become the physical man he has always hoped to be. After all that took place on this day, I am bracing myself for what the next two to three years will bring. I have a strong feeling we are in for a very bumpy ride.

December 4, 2005

The day before yesterday, Rhys suggested that Sundays might be better days for having his shot of testosterone.

"Do you think I'll get into trouble for switching days?" he asked.

His disposition is so innocent, so childlike, around this whole process. So this morning I arrived at Rhys' house around 9 am, to find him with all the anticipation of a kid on Christmas Eve. I went upstairs to wash my hands before my first round as... Nurse Ali, T-Momma! I came around the corner and caught view of Rhys, his back to me in the kitchen with his pants halfway down his ass, swabbing his butt cheek with the alcohol wipes I bought last minute at Walgreen's this morning.

I guess "eager" would be a gross understatement at this point?

He asked me, "Are you scared, Ali?"

Knowing full well that he and I are all about truth, I lied with a confidence that is born of 20 years of "best-interest-mothering."

"No," I assured him, "I am so entirely ready to do this."

I asked him if he was scared. His reply was quick and concise, "HELL YEAH!"

I knew that the longer it took to get the process underway, the more hesitant he would become. He took out a new syringe and uncapped the needle. We were given the type of needle that disposes of its own "sharp" by way of retreating back into the chamber of the syringe once used—Vanish Point. I stood by closely and watched. I had already decided that the best way through this entire transformation will be with Rhys calling all the shots (literally!). He gingerly stuck the needle into the rubber seal on the top end of the tiny brown glass bottle. Together, we figured out how to pull back the syringe enough to allow the thick, clear, liquid to drip into the chamber. Testosterone itself is very syrupy, as the nurse warned us it would be. That seems apropos to me, since all he gets each week is about a quarter of an inch of this dream serum. After all, this change can't come around fast enough for either of us, and part of me wants to pour the whole damn vial into some kind of "stud cocktail" and have him transform right in front of me. You have the visual here? Muscles so defined, so bulked out that they tear through his button-down work shirt...... the Incredible Hulk.

Rhys handed me the full syringe. I stretched the skin on his butt cheek with my thumb and forefinger, making it as taut as possible, just as the nurse instructed a week ago. At first gently, and then with more pressure, I slid the needle into his hesitant flesh, and pushed the testosterone out as quickly as I could.

Rhys gasped, "Oh! That stings a little, but it's good, you did good!"

I let out a breath, completely unaware of just how long I had been holding it in.

What a relief. I can do this. I can do this one important thing to be a part of his newness. A way for me to speak my love and support of his transition without uttering a word.

He pulled up his boxers with a satisfied grin and went upstairs to finish painting the bedroom.

December 6, 2005

Recently, a friend and I were having a conversation, during which I referenced to Rhys as "he" and "him," male pronouns. She commented on how "good" I am at using the correct pronouns for Rhys. I told her that it better be me who is the most aware of the words used around Rhys' transformation. I am silently called to set the precedent. I explained to her that for me it is merely an issue of respect.

She said that she has had some long conversations with Rhys and is starting to understand more and more clearly the journey he is on. She then went on to ask if she could get personal with me.

"Sure," I said, knowing what most likely would follow. Over the past few months, Rhys has individually told everyone in his life about his upcoming transition, and for the greater part, they have responded with respect, curiosity and immense support. After the first wave of "transgender curiosity" passes over the crowd, they are slowly turning their curiosity to me.

My friend asked me pointblank, "So, do you still consider yourself a lesbian if Rhys is transitioning to a man?"

I couldn't think of a more loaded question to have been asked. Is it even possible to make intelligible the sacred, intangible enigma that is my own sexuality? This is where *my* questions begin…

Why does our society seem to require any label on love?

When will the LGBTQ "community" become inclusive of all types of sexual expression and gender identity?

What the hell is a "lesbian" anyway? I have multitudes of friends who call themselves lesbians, and no two of them perceive each other as identical in belief. How can words and labels do anything but discriminate in a context that confines us?

Okay, okay, I am aware that I can only educate and inform one person at a time around this incredibly personal part of my life. So here in front of me sat my friend, and my opportunity to affirm what I know as my truth. I began by explaining that in the three years since I left my 20-year marriage to a non-trans (cisgender) male, I have questioned my sexuality more times than I want to account for.

Do I consider myself a lesbian? No. However, I have always been attracted to masculine women and people like Rhys.

My friend asked if I would put myself in the bisexual category then. I responded by saying maybe by the limited definitions of our culture, considering that I had been married to a non-trans male and am now with Rhys, a transgender man. I explained to her that transgender vocabulary is new to the general public and still evolving within the transgender community. Recently Rhys and I were reading an article that claimed "transsensual" is the latest term to be attached to a person who is attracted to, or partnered with, a transgender person. I know I don't want to be with a non-trans male, and I am not generally physically attracted to femme women for the most part. Allowing myself to be as vulnerable as I was comfortable doing, I told my friend that if I hadn't met Rhys, I would probably have chosen to be alone. She shared that she is struggling similarly with her sexual identity, and that she likes the word "omnisexual" to describe herself. I looked the word up, by splitting it in half. Omni means all pervasive, boundless, indiscriminate. (It also means having a mixed and varied diet, "able to eat anything"…hmmm.) Sexual is defined as erotic, procreative. I can see where this new buzzword would be suitable to many in the queer community.

When I discussed with my mother three years ago that I was questioning my sexuality, she quickly responded, "Well frankly, I don't like lesbians."

After attending numerous gatherings attended by women who identify with the title of lesbian I started to uncover a conundrum of sorts. Within the "lesbian" (Webster definition: a woman who loves other women) community, there are so many identities: bull dyke, butch, soft butch, granola, femme, queer femme, ultra femme.

And these only represent my (very) limited knowledge of the subject. I found myself questioning where, if at all, did I fit in? How could anyone say they don't like lesbians, and assume that means any one kind of woman? How could a person who lived through the horror of sexist discrimination during the 1950s, make such an ignorant statement? And how on earth did this extreme statement come out now at this point in my relationship with her? Never once in my upbringing did she have a negative or judging word to share about the LGBTQ community. Perhaps aging has propelled her backwards in her tolerance. Now obviously my mother is slightly shortsighted when it comes to the issue of diversity, but her statement definitely led me to a place of contemplation.

To me it seems an obsessive desire for some to describe a person's sexuality in linear terms. What I am painfully finding out is that there are no boundaries to where love leads us. What I feel about my own sexual self seems intangible, capable of defying the boundaries of language. My mother be damned (and she possibly is, but that's a whole different topic), but I realize through her shortsightedness, an evolution of sorts is positioning itself to take place here and now. After all, at what better point to start than with my own family of origin?

I feel the need to break this chain of ignorance through living my own truths…OUT LOUD.

December 7, 2005

Today Rhys told me he is PMS-ing on testosterone. I think he's supremely pissed about it, too. I'm thinking he wanted that whole bag of fun to go away with the first needle stick. No such luck. Rhys has suffered from severe and at times debilitating migraine headaches each and every month. This has been going on since he was in third grade. A constant and painful reminder that his body betrays his true spirit. Our hope is that these symptoms will diminish as the testosterone increases.

In the meantime, I am trying to rise above my normal allotment of daily energy to give him something special each day. I can't begin to understand what is going through his mind as the testosterone slowly invades his body all the way to the cellular level. I can see it in his eyes though. All the time… the anticipation, the frustration and the fear. Don't get me wrong, Rhys isn't afraid of taking the testosterone. No. Because on Sundays he's like a kid waiting for the ice cream truck. What he fears is that the whole change won't happen as quickly and as dramatically as he would like. What *I* fear is how much emotional stress one transman can handle.

Today we received a confirmation email from Dr. Brownstein's office in California for Rhys to have chest reconstruction surgery on February 8, 2006. We will be spending two weeks in San Francisco. Upon arriving, we'll have 24 hours before the surgery takes place the very next morning at 7AM. Rhys will be undergoing a bilateral prophylactic mastectomy with reconstruction. He will then be in my exclusive care for eight days, until the postop visit and the clearance to return home to Minneapolis. The costs will possibly reach over ten thousand dollars. The entire bill will be on his dime.

There are no words here, besides perhaps, I love him.

December 9, 2005

I want so badly to be able to remember and write everything that is said about this amazing experience. The questions we are asked are sometimes hilarious and other times invasive. Recently, my 16-year-old son, Eli, asked me if Rhys will be able to pee standing up now. An older woman and client asked Rhys if he will now be capable of getting a woman pregnant (!). Some people have no boundaries or insight enough to refrain from asking specific "genital questions." Can you imagine if we routinely asked each other in everyday conversation, details regarding our sex organs? A typical spur-of-the-moment meeting of an acquaintance might sound something like this:

"Hi Sue!"

"Hey John, haven't seen you in months, how big are your testicles these days?"

"Oh they're hangin' well, Sue, and I have frequent thoughts about your vagina. How is she by the way?"

I mean, COME ON! There's got to be a baseline level of respect, even in the face of this most unusual process Rhys is currently undergoing. I find myself becoming fiercely protective and private of both Rhys and his transformation. I am becoming less and less willing to respond to these questions, and when I do I find myself biting my wicked tongue, holding back the irritation that waits just behind my closed lips. I'm not sure there is some way to convey how emotionally painful this entire process has been for Rhys and myself up to now. He is so exhausted from being publicly scrutinized that our social life seems limited to the safety within the walls of our home. There isn't a day that passes—not a single day—without a comment from Rhys regarding his immense emotional pain around his being born transgender. All he wants and has desired for a very long time is to be whole in body and spirit—something that most of humanity takes for granted, to the extent that they can't even comprehend the idea of gender incongruence. There are things that Rhys will never be able to do (for example, catch up to his biological age in his new body, or father a child) no matter how many syringes of testosterone or how many scalpels pierce his skin.

The most hurtful thing as of today is when people fail to abide by Rhys' simple request to be addressed by male pronouns and his new name. After lovingly and vulnerably explaining his upcoming transition to each and every person in his life, Rhys' requests have routinely been met with blatant disregard. I have empathy with the need for time in this adjustment, but no tolerance for those who brazenly reply with, "Don't expect to me to make this change so easily."

It reminds me of my own process. About ten years ago, I decided to be called by my nickname and requested that no one use my full name from that point on. You would have thought that I had asked my family to learn to speak Portuguese backwards. They were insulted that I even made the request, and my Mom and brother outright refused (even to this day) to respect my wishes.

As time progresses and Rhys physically changes with the weekly doses of testosterone, he encounters situations where people use the wrong name or pronoun more frequently and this makes Rhys angry.

December 11, 2005

Dose 3. We painted walls all day. Redecorating Rhys' house appears to parallel the growing newness in his personal life. There is a sort of static excitement in the air every Sunday between the two of us. Sometimes it remains unspoken, but the looks of knowing that are exchanged between us add an energy to what is already an electric relationship. I am feeling ever more confident in this sudden role of "impromptu nurse." As Rhys drops his painter's pants to expose his wonderful ass, I wonder secretly how much he honestly trusts what I am about to do to him. If I were in the same position, my issues of control and hyper responsibility would force me into twisting my body in half at the mid-section in order to stick myself with the needle. But Rhys just stands there, waiting for his impending punishment. And unfortunately today, punishment is definitely what it was.

"OWWWW!" he moaned, *"What did you do?"* I recoiled by physically shrinking, "That really hurt this time," he complained.

He immediately saw regret on my face and apologized. I felt so awful. I can't stand being responsible for something so important that physically hurts him every time I do it. At the doctor's office, they showed us that it helps a lot to relax the leg on the same side as the injection. Rhys thinks that maybe it hurt more because he had been up and down a ladder all morning and into the afternoon. I'm not so keyed on all the variables involved in this process. I wish I could make this part less stressful; I sense the worst is yet to come. My six years of experience as a hospice caregiver will be more useful to me now than when I was actually with terminal clients. The reason is when I am emotionally invested as I am with Rhys, it's almost impossible to have boundaries around his pain.

Recently, I have been spending more time thinking about Rhys' impending chest reconstruction. I anticipate he will need more care, physically and emotionally, than he has had his entire life. I can already name my own obstacle in this: an overabundance of empathy. I need to find strength, even in the face of his pain and frustration. But most times when I look into his extraordinary eyes, I want to cry. There is a depth, a truth and a sorrow in his eyes that cannot be hidden from me, regardless of all his attempts to portray an "east-coast-badass" personality. I can see and feel the inner turmoil going on through the window of his eyes. When I have talked to close friends about my experiences working in hospice, the most common response has been, "I don't know how you do it. I know I couldn't do that work."

But the truth is, not one of us knows what we are capable of until we are faced with the actual challenge. With Rhys, I always knew I could. It just seems like the most authentic position to have with another human being: sharing the soul.

CHAPTER 2

Alterations

December 15, 2005

RHYS' VOICE IS ALREADY CHANGING. I dialed his number and the voice I heard was deeper and raspier than what I had previously recognized as my lover. But he *is* my lover: my lover on testosterone. Rhys' voice is very alluring to me; my body responds with its own yearnings each time I hear it. Voice is one of the most powerful pieces of recognition in human beings. So what will this mean for me as his voice changes? I'm afraid of the sudden flux in his defining physical characteristics. Rhys wears specific cologne, and every time I smell it anywhere, there is an olfactory memory response that belongs only to him. If he were to wear new cologne, it would not (at first) affect me in the same manner as the old one. Of course I'll still recognize him but there will be a change in that recognition. Will my body still yearn to be near him?

As I notice this slow but sure change in him, I am realizing something else: a definite change in me. And it's a big one. As a woman, I have always looked upon other women with an unspoken understanding of our commonality. In general, women treat one another differently than they treat those of the "male gender." Ever since the day I met Rhys, I have been more responsive to his masculine energy than to any other part of him. He was physically living in the body of a female, but his masculine energy was evident within twenty seconds of meeting him. Now I am acutely aware that with his transformation, I am also changing. With the growing level of testosterone in his body, my perception of him has shifted to perceiving him as indisputably male. And honestly, I act differently around men. For one, I will not divulge as much of myself in the presence of a man. So now, when Rhys sweetly begs me to share a secret thought, I am less likely to give in to his pleas. A woman has to have her secrets. There is a division of sorts. When Rhys was living in the physical body of a female, I knew on a basic physical level that we had a minimal understanding of one another. But now he is changing into a physical male, and inevitably I feel like that separates us somehow. I have no idea what it is like to experience the physical attributes of being male, yet, day-by-day, this is Rhys' experience. As I write, I also view this as a positive change; I am seeing Rhys at the core of what he has always felt. What was once intangible has now come into the realm of the physical. My energy is changing in response.

I strongly believe there has been a shift in the pheromones, and Rhys is suddenly at a greater advantage than he ever was before. I find myself flustered around him, and I have noticed the same in other women. Even the woman who owns the restaurant where we dine at least once a week has begun to blush when chatting with Rhys at our table. It's so interesting to be able to observe women from the perspective of his change. I often tease Rhys that when he walks through a room, women's panties slide down to their ankles without them even knowing it. He is alarmingly handsome.

I'm beginning to fear not what will be *gained* through this transition, but what for me may inevitably be *lost*.

December 18, 2005

I'm starting to feel at ease with the T shots with each passing week. It's actually beginning to feel natural to be participating in this Sunday morning ritual of delayed puberty. The changes that are clearly evident to me so far are: the deepening of Rhys' voice (it actually cracks at times), and the widening of his jaw. It's ever so slight a change, but it's definitely there. I am thrilled for him that change is occurring. He, however, is irritated with the fact that this change cannot and is not happening quickly enough. With me Rhys is very vulnerable, and yet I am aware that there is much that he does not share…with anyone. I wish I could jump into his thoughts once in a while. Not for too long though, because I don't think it's easy to be Rhys. Perhaps if I could, it would help me in my quest to educate the world (and myself), on how to be respectful of a transgender person. I'll be the first to admit, with great humility and sadness, that I am also guilty of carelessness around using the appropriate words with Rhys. Every day, he and I are inundated with opportunities to correct people who address us as "ladies," or who unfortunately call Rhys, "Ma'm." He talks about his pain and frustration. He gets angry. Really angry. He contemplates why we live in a binary gender society where there are no words yet to address a he/she transgender person. "He" still sounds new and awkward to Rhys, but "she" is an affront to his character. All of this is intimately and lovingly shared with me, his lover and confidant, with a trust that comes from deep in his soul. I meet this trust with honor and boundless respect.

Today, however, I fucked up. HUGE. To sum it up with the greatest impact: I added a careless "girl" on to the end of a sentence I spoke to Rhys. I don't know where it came from. Some remote part of my brain that speaks unconsciously for me when I am not fully present in each moment? I don't honestly know. I truly don't see Rhys as feminine in any way. The word didn't connect my feelings to it. But it was too late once spoken. Too fucking late.

How can you become a time traveler in moments of severe betrayal, to go backwards just one word and be more aware? Truth is, you can't. The remorse I felt was immediate and all consuming. Rhys only said, "Give me a minute."

But after a silent hour had passed, I knew his pain warranted longer than a minute towards forgiveness. He said nothing to me the rest of the whole day except, "I just can't wrap my brain around this, I'm deeply hurt." I felt a heaviness descend over my body—a blanket woven of lead and shame.

I wanted to talk to Rhys right away: to tell him how sad I was and how I don't see him as a girl. How ridiculous. Of all words . . . *girl*?!

I write these entries partly because I have found no other account of the transgender experience through the eyes of a lover. I have found no resources to help me. Nothing to make comparison to. I sometimes feel that I am under a scorching magnifying glass in this transition with him. He gives me so much. He notices everything. (A characteristic in our relationship that was painfully absent in my previous relationships.) I feel it is somewhat my responsibility to set the precedent for how to address and speak to Rhys. I truly sense there is no room for error here. And yet, being human and fallible, it is in my nature to make an error occasionally. The thing is, here is a situation where I have been given the gift of opportunity: the opportunity to painfully rise above mediocrity of mind and speak well thought-out ideas and words. It is an imperative call to consciousness.

It took until the next day for Rhys to confront me. It wasn't easy. The depth of my pain from having hurt him so much had profoundly changed me. In general, I don't consider myself to be careless with my words. In fact, in social situations I often find myself an observer, eaves-dropping on other's conversations. I have even devised a game that can secretly be played in any social situation. When meeting and conversing with a new person, I try to see how much information I can obtain about them and how little they can in turn, learn about me. Some people are so incredibly self-absorbed it doesn't take much skill to win at this game. So anyway, that word had spilled out of me—*girl*—unexpected and unwelcome like an audible fart in church.

I gave many, many tears and much thought to this situation. Rhys said he just couldn't wrap his brain around it. Truth be told, neither could I. The more I thought about what happened, the more I became aware of how important our language is. What a gift we have in our everyday speech. Yet, in that gift there is also a great responsibility to use words consciously with love and respect. If this standard were the social norm there would be no verbal discrimination, no racial slurs, and more than likely a greater sense of understanding. I am beginning to realize the magnitude of the situation I am in with Rhys. I boldly told a friend about my error, and her response was, "There has to be some room for error in this transition, after all, we are only human."

But if I am really acting and speaking from a place of consciousness, then being human is no longer a fair excuse for carelessly hurting my lover.

December 22, 2005

My opportunity came of its own timing. I was pulling some food out of the fridge for us, when I said, "I feel so awful about what happened the other day. I was out doing errands with Chelsae (my daughter), and feeling wired (as being with my 20-year-old daughter often does to me). When I came back to your house, I continued speaking to you in the language Chelsae and I had used. I wasn't exactly present with you," I tried to explain from my heart, "I was careless with my words and didn't think about what I was saying, and by the time I said it there was no turning back."

Rhys listened intently, and I began to see softness and empathy toward me in his eyes.

But I wasn't finished.

"What's important to me is that you know my carelessness truly is no reflection of how I perceive you. And I know that from your perspective it might sound totally different, but honestly there was no malicious intention behind my words."

Rhys was quiet for a while, and then he spoke, "I knew in my head that something else must have been a factor in your carelessness. I kept saying to myself, '…but this is Ali, and I know her, heart and soul.' I knew you would never intend to hurt me, and that's how I got to forgiveness so quickly. But I was shaking I really wanted to throw up. I wanted to pull away from you … to run away."

He continued, "Then my rational thoughts came through and reminded me of all that we have with each other. That's how I knew I had to stay in this with you, and let you know how much it hurt. How much your words hurt me."

Still straining to hold back the weighted tears on my lower lids, I told Rhys how much I learned from this experience. I still want to defend myself and say I can't be perfect. But perfection isn't what this is about. It's about being conscious and truly being present in every situation in my life. I realize that this call to constant awareness with Rhys has crossed over into my daily practice of listening and communicating with each and every person I interact with in my day.

Growth hurts like a bitch, but in the end I know I'm better for it.

December 25, 2005

How fitting for a transgender guy to wake up on Christmas morning and get a shot of testosterone in his ass cheek as a gift. Each time I give Rhys a dose of the testosterone, I get pretty emotional. He told me today (after the short lived, initial pain of the injection) that I was doing an amazing job of giving him the testosterone. The dam broke; I started to cry.

"This is just so important to me," I began. "Along with giving birth to the kids, this is the most important thing I have ever done!" He grabbed me and held me while I cried tears of relief.

Rhys' voice continues to deepen, and yesterday he introduced me to his first testosterone induced pimple! That's right, he's getting zits, just like every other horny, 16 year-old boy. So far, I am unaffected by this, except for how it bugs Rhys. And please believe me when I tell you, it bugs the shit out of him! He has great skin and he doesn't want to sacrifice his complexion, his hairline or his waistline for the masculine features he desperately desires. We have been forewarned; some of the possible side effects of testosterone include acne, hair loss (in the wrong place), hair gain (in the very below the waist places) and weight gain. Only coincidence I suppose then, that these are the three things Rhys fears the most! I have become aware of how important it is to consistently reassure Rhys of his continued physical attractiveness through this time of change.

I asked him if there was anything he really wanted for Christmas since he hadn't asked for anything specific.

He replied with an assurance that sent chills through my body, "I WANT A PENIS."

I respected him too much to respond.

December 29, 2005

Washing clothes at the local laundromat. A mundane, everyday activity that we have done week after week. This is the way I imagine news stories begin that end tragically in a massacre at a local McDonald's.

A disheveled man walked in and prepared his sleeping bags for the huge industrial dryers. I, on the other hand, was enjoying the flirtatious nature of Rhys in the most ordinary of activities. The way it turned out, this man's sleeping bags were too big for the size of the dryers and the nylon fabric slowly melted as the machine heated inside. We could smell the acrid odor of melting plastic. The guy was very obviously mentally ill and apparently vagrant. The sleeping bags he was washing were no doubt vital to his existence. As he pulled his few possessions from the dryer, he regarded Rhys and me with a deranged look that was worthy of a Stephen King movie. He began to blame us, specifically Rhys, for ruining his stuff.

He yelled, calling Rhys a "faggotman" and he demanded to see his identification. The man was physically blocking the only exit of the building. Rhys grabbed his laundry, "We gotta get the hell out of here!" he told me. The situation was quickly escalating, and I was really afraid for our safety. An attendant came over and distracted the guy long enough to allow us to pass by him without his noticing.

As we bolted for the door, Rhys yelled at the man, "I'm not a man, just so you know I'm trans!"

That's when the vagrant man began to move towards us as he yelled,

"Then you're a female faggot! Get that female faggot's I.D.!"

We flew out of there as fast as our fear could carry us. As we pulled up in front of Rhys' house, I got out of my car and realized he was shaking. We decided to call the police, and waited in his truck for them to show up. It was at this very point that I became aware of how even in the midst of chaos and the face of personal danger it was important for Rhys to claim his "transness" to the general public. He's getting bold. Here we were, literally running away from an apparently mentally ill man, who had God knows what in his army belt with multiple pockets, and Rhys felt it important to stop and clarify in the face of personal harm, his gender identity. I love this man.

It would appear everything he does is a turn-on to me. Lately, the trans identity is poised at the tip of Rhys' tongue waiting to roll out at any and every opportunity. When I'm in the presence of this self-proclamation, I am thrilled at the urgency for him to claim his newness. Bold would be an understatement; Rhys has balls of steel.

December 31, 2005

According to what I've read, many people who identify as transgender struggle heavily with depression. Rhys has informed me on a few very vulnerable occasions that the thought of suicide is often of great comfort to him. Doing my best to hide my feelings of horror at this thought, I listen to his feelings that usher him to this place. The daily pain of living as a man within the body of a female is conducive to self-hatred and depression. Rhys seems to take it moment-by-moment fairly regularly. But then something triggers this somber reality, and he gets sucked under with a force that drains him of his ability to stay positive. He pulls away from me and doesn't want to be seen. But as Rhys has pointed out, persistence is my strongpoint. I will do everything in my power to support him through these crises of self-loathing. It's incredibly painful for me to witness this in him. He is so attractive, so loving, so compassionate and true. He is all the man I could possibly handle, and that is exactly how I perceive him each and every day. And yet none of that matters when he is this depressed. I wish for just a moment he could have the ability to enter into my perception and see himself through me. As with anyone who loves a person suffering from depression, I struggle to know how to help. Mostly I just feel fucking helpless. At times, I believe I was born not into the innocence of a child, but into the seemingly eternal role of mother. Sometimes this characteristic rides on a slippery slope for me. My desire to make everything right crosses over into making everyone right. My difficult task as of late is to know where I can help, and where to stop so that I can help myself.

January 4, 2006

Rhys is miserable, literally and figuratively. Today, he woke with "A wicked migraine." This is a bad on so many levels. First and foremost, he is in an incredible amount of pain.

His quickly deepening voice cannot begin to hide the suffering in his body. Second, a migraine often heralds the onslaught of PMS.

PMS for a trans man is like mixing oil and water, or toothpaste and orange juice, the combination doesn't mix well. Remember watching that skit on Sesame Street when you were four? "One of these things is not like the others; one of these things does not belong here!"

Need I say more?

Rhys needs to rid his body of this physical betrayal. The doctor told him that this stuff would stop within the first month of taking testosterone. But now two months have passed, and his body's nemesis has returned yet again with a vengeance. The irony of our relationship is this: I, the aptly titled, "ultra-femme," haven't had a period in 16 years (due to a not-so-fun bout with ovarian cancer in my mid-20s). Rhys, on the other, other hand, a masculine, somewhat soft butch trans man has to deal with the monthly cycle of a woman, while at the same time transitioning into a man.

WHAT THE FUCK?

Mother Nature has some explaining to do when this is all said and done. I never thought I would say this, but if I could take his monthly shit from him and do it for him, at this point, I know I would. He has a much anticipated appointment with the doctor on Monday, I'm sure Rhys will be insisting on a testosterone increase.

January 5, 2006

As impossible as I would have thought it to be yesterday, Rhys' pain got worse today. Physically yes, but emotionally it's like a landmine. He is so miserable. Swollen chest, bloated body, nonexistent energy level, but by far the most detrimental to his well-being is the petulant nature of his hopelessness. There is no "good" way for me to act around Rhys when he is like this. Being cute and full of adoration was strike one.

He has so much self-loathing going on right now my compliments only irritate him further. All the issues are in an unsettled state in his mind magnified to a point where they don't all fit into one room. He seems determined for me to know that I can never understand the depth of his pain, and he does this in his own in-your-face-Jersey style.

The thing is I would never venture to claim anything close to understanding this issue. I try to step around all the jagged shards of shame and anger and self-loathing which protect him from outsiders.

Unfortunately, this can be hard to do without inevitably slicing myself wide open on a misstep. What I wish Rhys could understand about me, is that it's pretty rough right now. Day to day, there is the stress of living with the constant fear of someone referring to Rhys in a feminine pronoun. His tolerance for this is quickly diminishing and often the response is, "Could you please not use the term 'ladies', because I am *transgender* and that word deletes me from the rest of society. And after all, we are in Uptown which is a LGBTQ community."

It's gotten to the point where I now do an internal cringe before a wait person even opens their mouth. Standing in support of Rhys has never been a difficult task for me, but the situation that he is currently experiencing requires more than support. He needs gentle understanding and a vigilant respect for his incredible process. Again, I would benefit greatly from some pittance of information on this topic. So I think that maybe I'll just start a conversation with a few random girlfriends and acquaintances: "Hey, you know when your boyfriend gets his period two months after it should have stopped, how do you deal with his feelings?"

I'm sure someone out there can relate to my situation...yeah, right. I feel so alone in this lately. There are many new resources for transgender individuals: support groups, clinics, therapists, even places to hang out together. But if I walked into any one of those places, my fear is that I would be ignored into invisibility. As the transgender community becomes more prevalent in our society, the resources around their needs must grow in accordance. But what about the needs of those who are trying to support their partners and lovers through the often hellish experience of transitioning? I can't seem to find my place in this tiny subculture. There is a Program in Human Sexuality at the University of Minnesota that Rhys is hooking up with. He will be participating in a support group for transitioning FTMs (female-to-male transsexuals). I already feel a little on the outside. I don't expect him to tell me everything that enters into his brain, but I wish I could be privy to what he would say around other FTMs in transition. I know for sure it would be different than anything he would talk to me about.

There are some chat groups online that are oriented toward partners of trans people. So far I haven't found my niche. Often, when I receive the incoming threads of dialogue they are void of anything regarding a transgender partner. There's been a lot more "chat" about who is dating who, and I have noticed that there is definitely a social aspect to these online groups that goes beyond supporting and educating each other. This may be a perfect fit for some, but I have so much more I need to say. Ironically, I have found comfort as of late on a chat group for FTMs. At times, I feel a peculiar sense of voyeurism, but what's interesting is that the trans guys are much more honest and raw about their entire experience. There is no topic that is taboo. By reading these daily threads of dialogue, I am learning so much about the experience of other trans men. This information helps me to understand what is going on with Rhys and what I can expect in the future. It gives me comfort and a sense of hope that this void I have entered may not be so dark after all.

Because of where we are in the newness of Rhys' transition, as a couple we are still quite a topic of interest for most people, and therefore, I feel any personal information I divulge in the hopes of getting support just feeds the growing level of curiosity. I need a private place where my feelings can be spit out right onto the floor and those witnessing will not recoil or bat an eye. What I've learned is that many relationships don't make it through the transitioning process. Could that be because there is almost no support for those of us in love with trans people?

January 8, 2006

It's verifiable and evident to the naked eye, Rhys has a mustache! And let me just add right here, he wears it very well. The minute I noticed it today I couldn't help from staring at his upper lip. I was "transfixed," and even with my best effort at listening we both knew, he and I, that my attention was in hyper-focus at this welcomed new addition. I prattled on about it constantly, because Rhys tends to focus on what *isn't* happening, instead of what *is*. This is no revelation; he is self-proclaimed as "incorrigible by nature." I believe at this place in our journey my positivity bears more weight than ever. Don't get me wrong, I'm not just blowing smoke up his ass, but he sometimes needs to be reminded that there have been visible (and audible!) changes in the past seven weeks. Rhys doesn't notice as readily as I. I make a parallel to a woman during pregnancy (which Rhys will not appreciate on any level): day by day, the changes are so gradual, so minute, and then one day you wake up and there is a huge physical change that you didn't see there before. The problem that I feel I am sometimes facing is that no amount of flattery or compliments regarding Rhys' newborn masculine traits can ever replace the fact that he was not born into a male body. Truly, only words with shock value can justify how much emotional pain Rhys suffers from and around this loss. The odd thing is it's not a loss for me. I don't think of him as not being in the body of a male. Not even right now. He's just Rhys to me. And that fulfills what I need and want in an emotional and physical relationship. His energy is what I feel, and it takes me places that flesh has never even ventured close to taking me. That being said, there is a division of sorts growing between us and it all appears to center around his growing sense of loss.

January 10, 2006

Can a day get any more exciting for a trans guy than to have his testosterone levels increased by the doctor? Well, we certainly don't think so at this point. I was anxious to ask my new list of questions, and even more so, to learn that nothing I've done (in regards to giving the injections) has been life threatening up to this point. I asked the nurse if the tiny little bubbles that refused to move out of the syringe chamber were cause for alarm. I needed to put the urban legend to rest once and for all. Unfortunately for me, the visit took a quick turn into a language with which I am not fluent. Rhys is a doctor and realizing his level of understanding of cellular biology, his own doctor began to explain what was happening to him in direct medical terminology. Now, please don't get me wrong here, I can go a few rounds of water soluble lipids and free testosterone levels with the best of them. But this little meeting of the minds quickly became the meeting of THEIR minds. Lacking the required skills in shorthand, there was much information that went unrecorded for later reflection.

Rhys continues to bemoan the fact that his body isn't changing fast enough. Perhaps not for him, but it's plenty fast for me.

After the visit to the doctor, Rhys had scheduled a mandatory appointment to see a therapist. In order to participate in a support group for FTMs, he must have two appointments (paid for out of pocket, of course), with a psychologist at the University of Minnesota's Program in Human Sexuality. This is just one tiny jump through a seemingly unending circus of proverbial hoops for him to transition. Rhys would love to shove this hoop right up somebody's ass.

Driving up to the sterile glass office building, I contemplated what direction this labyrinth of gender discovery—or recovery, depending on perception—would take us. We found ourselves in a waiting room with a random group of others, and when Rhys went to register at the receptionist window, I glanced around at the various pieces of literature lying around. I was more than delighted to find alternative magazines on the tables that spoke to the LGBTQ community— *The Advocate, OUT, Girlfriends*. On the wall were racks lined with pamphlets on services offered by the program. As I looked closer, I noticed information on sexual health for couples, lesbians and gays, and multiple publications on the AIDS crisis. Scanning the wall, I grabbed a pamphlet on transgender programs, when out of the corner of my eye I read the next pamphlet title, "Sexual Addiction and the Sex Offender."

Oh my fucking God!

You mean to tell me that the University of Minnesota's highly touted program for the transgender community is housed in the same place as the program for pedophiles and sex offenders?! I was instantly insulted, then enraged. I found a chair to camp out in where I could clearly observe the comings and goings of all who entered the office.

Meanwhile, Rhys was called back for his "therapy" by a young woman who looked like she just got her degree last weekend. It gave me the opportunity to fume a little more about the clinic. When Rhys came out, he told me that it went as well as could be expected. I think he meant that it went as well as it could for a trans man divulging the most private part of his existence to a complete stranger who is the gatekeeper holding his golden ticket into a trans support group.

January 21, 2006

Rhys has been sick with a viral flu for seven days. Not the least bit fun. He needs to get better fast, because we leave for San Francisco and chest surgery in 16 days. I realized today that I don't really believe Rhys is FTM, (female to male). It can't be the correct title for someone who was never female in the first place. I have relabeled Rhys as TTM; transgender to male. I ask this: can breasts and a vagina truly be the qualifying indicator of a woman? Obviously not, as my trans boy would be the first to agree. Can you even imagine that it was common practice in childbirth as recently as the 1960's, for the delivering doctor to determine the biological sex of a child born intersexed with evidence of both male and female genitals? How inhumane can we possibly be? Before the child even has an inkling of being masculine or feminine, the gender is determined by which sex organ is more easily disposed of surgically. How many people are walking around without any knowledge that this "procedure" was performed on them within minutes of their birth, and without the knowledge or consent of their parent? Are there perhaps some gay men who are actually masculine females? And how many butch women or bull dykes are truly male at birth?

Why does our society continue to grow and embrace the idea of so many body-mind connections, but not when it comes to transgender people? Perhaps love has jaded me, because I fail to see the strangeness of my situation with Rhys. I often marvel at how unbelievably different each of our bodies are. If you want to understand this better, I have a great experiment for you to try. Find a diversely populated public place where you can be somewhat inconspicuous, and sit somewhere that you can closely observe people as they pass. My favorite spot is the train depot in Chicago, but any mall or airport will do. Choose a body part to focus on. Just for shits and giggles, let's say the ass. Sit and behold how many different shapes and sizes asses come in, and you will inevitably find that no two are alike. It is probably the most juvenile, and at the same time the most eye-opening experiment you will ever perform. As you sit there observing this "multitude of ass," you'll be amazed at how different each and every body is. If it's possible for the exterior of the human body to come in such an abundance of variances, then where and when did the rightwing, fundamentalist movement decide that if the brain does the same, it's blatant sin?

I remember watching a program on public television once about how the brain and the body cannot be separated. This is a scientific fact. So what the hell? It doesn't seem like a person would have to be an expert in human sexuality to understand the transgender person. Every single one of us is born with our own personal road map of DNA. No two women or men are exactly the same, even in the case of identical twins. Yet, as a culture, we still have the archaic belief that certain body parts denote women, and others men. It appears that anytime the body parts in question are directly related to human sexuality there is an inevitable backlash of name calling, bible thumping and hate crimes. Yet, if a child is born with ears too large for the proportion of its head, there are surgeons running from every direction ready to correct those babies' ears. What the hell? Understanding gender is so incredibly worthy of its complexity, I can only hope that my future grandchildren will have the freedom to choose and express their own gender identity. Until then we suffer through the consequences of our culture's self-created hell.

January 22, 2006

The actual injection thing is becoming a routine part of my life. If asked, I don't know whether or not Rhys would respond with a similar answer. I try to imagine being on his side of the needle on a weekly basis. It occurs to me that he trusts me beyond anyone in any relationship I have ever known.

Following this arduous week of Rhys having a flu that kicked him on his Irish-Italian ass, we moved to a level of intimacy that I had never known before, not ever in my entire life. I have never witnessed him so incredibly ill. His face flush with fever, his eyes glazed over with overheating, I am reminded of my children when they had those wicked viruses passed between schoolmates. But to watch a grown man flat on his back, squeeze tears away that run down the sides of his face and into his ears! Such a mockery of the high energy instigator I know and love. I feel indispensable right now, and our level of trust keeps upping the ante.

January 24, 2006

Conversations between Rhys and me are becoming ever increasingly raw. There is actually no more fitting word: RAW. As Rhys bends over weekly to receive the hormone that whatever higher power so carelessly overlooked, I am observing the transformation that Rhys predicted for himself. He is beginning to strike a balance within which affects every aspect of who he is. Out of the blue, he says that he has been thinking about the trip to San Francisco (two weeks from today), and he feels at peace—actually full of joy—about his decision to have chest reconstruction surgery.

An interesting side note: Our good friend is having breast reduction surgery exactly one week after Rhys' chest reconstruction. She says her breasts are a size GG and make her feel like a porn star on her five-foot-two-inch frame. She and Rhys joke about the irony of their upcoming surgeries when they get together. Our friend has felt for many years that her breasts get in the way of her self-identity. (Not to mention her tits are breaking her back.) There is a consistent incongruence for both of them. She has the freedom to choose a surgery *with* health benefits, so I can't help but wonder, why can't Rhys? Why can't Rhys decide what his body requires for his own sense of congruency…his wholeness?

January 26, 2006

Just when I think things can't possibly get more twilight zone-ish, I find myself in a situation where I am waiting for Rod Serling to step out from the shadows: "What you are about to see…."

Such an occasion showed itself today while Rhys and I were at the University of Minnesota for his second appointment with a psychologist. Rhys had been contemplating how to get me into the session with him, something he told me he was trying to do, and true to form he delivered on his word. I was allowed to accompany him, thankfully, instead of perching myself for the hour in the not-so-friendly environment of the waiting room. The young, soft spoken psychologist had an inviting office decorated with literature on diversity, Rainbow Pride posters, and a small personal library of LGBTQ books that rivaled none I've ever seen. She began right off by informing Rhys that a new support group for FTMs was beginning in two weeks, and he was invited to take part. I could see the excitement in his eyes, and deservedly so. After all, where the hell *are* all the trans people in Minneapolis? It has become clear to me that it is through groups such as these that Rhys will find some camaraderie. I can't imagine having to pay eighty dollars twice a month just to meet people with whom I identify. This however, appears to be the predicament for Rhys. As we sat together facing the psychologist in her small office, she handed us an invitation to a transgender potluck dinner for people in the FTM group and their partners.

I immediately traveled mentally to that place and time and imagined myself walking into a room filled with transgender people like Rhys. I wondered what they would think of me, more than I would of them.

A potluck.

A transgender potluck?

Hmmmm…

Could that possibly resemble the church basement functions that were an unfortunate part of my younger years? Would I walk into the room and find the square card table with white stick-on nametags, "Hi, I'm _____!"

Perhaps at the transgender potluck, you get to be more creative with the fill-in-the-blank part.

For me it might say, "Hi, I'm not a straight girl!", or perhaps even more interesting would be, "Hi, I'm pretending to be an adult!" My first thought was that there would be no way Rhys would want to be so vulnerable as to enter a potluck full of trans people, but we'll see.

When asked if there was anything we wanted to discuss or add, I couldn't hold my tongue about the literature on the pedophile stuff tossed among the pamphlets on LGBTQ information in the waiting room.

"I would like to make a comment on the way things are set up in your waiting room," I cautiously began. "It's shocking to me that in a place where sexual offenders and pedophiles are receiving mandatory treatment, transgender people are also coming to find resources for support. Does this program look upon sexual deviants and those who are born transgender as equivalent?"

As I finished, Rhys interjected, "As a trans person, I represent a group of people who are sometimes victimized by those in sex offender programs, and being put in the same area of this clinic is offensive to me."

The therapist reassured us that the people who are employed by this program do not feel that being trans identified is a form of sexual deviancy or dysfunction. She also assured us she would bring our comments to her coworkers. What struck me during our discussion is it became clear by her facial expression that no one, likely not even herself, had considered the issue up until now.

DISTURBING!

Somehow I can't help but think that this gross oversight constitutes a HUGE misunderstanding of the trans community in the very place that they are led to believe they are the most understood. Is anyone paying attention here? Having first-hand experience being victimized by a pedophile in my own childhood, I personally believe that pedophiles and sex offenders should have facilities separate from LGBTQ persons seeking support. Of all groups to put together, sex offenders and the LGBTQ community?

SERIOUSLY?

Do I have to be rude to make this even clearer? Would we as a society (that largely considers pedophilia at the top of the "list of sexual taboos") ever put therapy for children who have been sexually molested in the same office as therapy for sex offenders? Is it just me here, or is there a giant purple elephant in the middle of that waiting room that everyone is trying to avoid? It is exactly this kind of insidious, subliminal discrimination that helps perpetuate the belief that something is wrong with transgender people. My belief is that the change must begin at the source, the organizations offering services to the transgender community. If Rhys and I miss a single opportunity to have our voices heard, the cumulative effect will be increased ignorance. The exact opposite of what we hope to achieve around Rhys and his process. More importantly, if the organizations that are working for the trans community (and for the entire LGBTQ community as a whole) are not aware and sensitive, we will have a serious problem.

The Program in Human Sexuality at the University of Minnesota is well respected, and it's currently the only program of its kind in Minnesota. Does it not seem ridiculous to have convicted sex offenders frequenting the same office? Someone there will definitely be getting a phone call from me. I refuse to be lulled into complacency by the promise of my concern "being mentioned to the rest of the staff." This road I travel with Rhys is as difficult as any I have ever been on, especially with sexual predators inadvertently added in as part of the experience.

January 31, 2006

The other day, Rhys shaved his face for the very first time. He told me he couldn't sleep, so he got up in the middle of the night and he shaved. The brain of a man. I had noticed something vaguely different about his face when I first saw him, but I didn't immediately pinpoint that he was clean shaven. He looks so great. His face is gradually broadening, and he is getting thicker facial hair on his upper lip and chin. I find myself staring at him all the time.

What is truly amazing for me, is being on the inside of Rhys' emotional process—literally, at the core—with all of what is happening.

One week from today we are leaving for San Francisco, and toward his state-of-the-art body. I honestly don't quite know what to think right now. We are taking it one day at a time at his point. For example, Rhys is still smoking "the occasional cigar," and I feel powerless against his small acts of self-destruction. (It's best not to smoke anything prior to any type of surgery.) I have arrived at a new place of self-preservation in the face of this nasty habit. I am not him; furthermore, I cannot stop him from doing whatever he will to his own body. He insists that he will be healed and ready to return to work within the two weeks of our stay in San Francisco.

"Mind over matter," he states with great confidence.

February 1, 2006

Something isn't right. My T-man got his fucking period yet again. On the last visit to the doctor we were told that this shouldn't be happening. So she increased Rhys' testosterone dose and sent us on our way. Rhys was thrilled to know that he had seen the last external signs of the female reproductive cycle. So what the hell is happening now, I don't know. I resign to remain calm and positive, thinking and acting in a proactive manner. But I honestly don't want to. My real thought is more along the lines of, "Why the hell can't one part of this process be easy? Isn't it tribulation enough for him to have to suffer financial and physical sacrifice to acquire his full, true identity?"

I just hung up from talking to Rhys, and he is feeling heavy with defeat. As the shadowy stubble of his upper lip increases in thickness and color, his body rhythm continues to act as though estrogen rules the day. It seems like he can't see beyond the moment of this hindrance. So tomorrow he will call the doctor's office and hope for luck to be on his side. Nothing I say seems to salve the wound of this returning pest. If anything, this process keeps teaching me the importance of my listening skills. Half the time whatever I say is too much anyway.

As more and more people rally and support our upcoming journey to San Francisco, I am feeling increasingly anxious about my role as sole care provider. Not that I will have trouble rising to the task, but I will be out there doing it ALL by myself. To allay my anxiety, I am gathering email addresses from friends so I can update everyone on Rhys' progress and perhaps gain some welcome support when needed.

February 5, 2006

Two more days of Rhys and his breasts! Monday, Tuesday, De-boob-day. I am ready to leave and embark with him on his transformation process. We saw the movie *Trans America* this afternoon. It was playing at the Uptown Theatre, a progressive, LGBTQ friendly, indie film theatre in Minneapolis. Thank God for the Uptown. Trans people were everywhere, as well as a few Bears and gay couples. It was so beautiful. I would love to exist in a world where love was just accepted for what it is, no matter who it is.

As we were waiting for the film to begin, I told Rhys that I am going to miss being identified as a couple in the LGBTQ community after his chest surgery is complete. The general public will most likely then perceive us as an average white heterosexual couple. It's an oxymoron of sorts, in that Rhys has wanted nothing less than this freedom his entire life. And yet, we are still most comfortable and feel most supported by the LGBTQ community. If we were to go to a "gay party" now, we would not in all probability be as accepted by the community as we would if we were lesbians. It will be an interesting (and painful) process to find new friendships where we are accepted for being exactly who we are.

Tomorrow night Rhys goes to his first FTM support group meeting. In all honesty, I'm pretty envious of this opportunity he has to meet other people in the transgender community. I wish I could be privy to what they're talking about....

I am exhausted thinking about how Rhys will handle his impending physical surgery. At times I wonder if I think too much for my own mental wellbeing.

February 7, 2006

We arrived in San Francisco at about 2 pm this afternoon. Not without incident, mind you. Rhys is being stared at while we're waiting to board the plane in Minneapolis...

A May-December looking couple:

Him: silver haired, well dressed suit, mid-60s.

Her: Not-as-young-as-she-looks blonde in a pink blazer, far too interested in looking at other women.

A gentleman makes a quiet yet audible comment to his female companion, nodding in our direction, "There's a couple of lesbians."

Of course I know better than to say anything to Rhys, but I ignore my better judgment and tell him what I just overheard. Rhys goes off on how he is going to set the record straight with the guy when we get on the plane, and I commence on a mini-prayer vigil praying that we aren't seated anywhere near these people.

So much for that, as Murphy's Law would dictate, they are seated directly across the aisle from us.

As Rhys passes, he leans in close to the guy, and quips, "Just for future reference, I'm transgender, not a lesbian."

The man was obviously shaken and put on his best, I-don't-know-a-thing-about-what-you-are-saying face.

It doesn't matter though because he knows in his own conscience that he's been officially busted. The rest of the flight was uneventful since the woman and her apparent "sugah daddy" did everything in their power not to look in our direction. I hope to God it gave them both stiff necks.

I find myself getting nervous around Rhys when he is confronted with people's ignorance. If I truly tapped into the emotion behind my discomfort, it's this: I am afraid that someone might be crazy enough to physically hurt him or us. Rhys is more confrontational than anyone I have ever known. His New Jersey roots have taught him well. And me, coming from a family of "smile-and-pretend-we-are-perfect," I am learning to be more comfortable with people around me having their voice. But it's still an unfamiliar experience for me every time it happens. I am from Minnesota after all.

We quickly found our way around San Francisco and were thrilled to realize the row house we rented for our stay was peaceful and conveniently located. It literally sat right on the corner of Castro Street.

After dropping our bags off, we ventured to the Rainbow Co-op. It was amazing. Not only the co-op itself, but the people, OH MY GOD! There were transgender people all over the place. I wasn't aware as trans people anonymously walked passed me. Rhys pointed out a trans man who was obviously already on testosterone and had undergone chest reconstruction and he looked incredible. I was filled with a rush of anticipation for Rhys' continuing transition.

Everywhere we went that day, Rhys was getting the avid attention of gay men. As we sat near the window eating dinner at a quaint little oyster bar in Castro, the men passing on the street were ogling my trans boy. God bless him, he was loving it. That was until a short, muscular man with a shaved head actually stopped in his tracks directly in front of us and smiled and waved at Rhys. Instantly turning the color of a blush wine, Rhys leaned forward so the guy couldn't see (sexualize) him. In that moment, I turned to look at the wanna-be-lover-on-the-street to catch him winking at my boyfriend! What a riot! And it continued on from there. A man at the bar disclosed that it would be worth the wait to order our dinner when the specials were offered. As we got to talking, he proved to be a knowledgeable and friendly native. Rhys was enjoying sharing information with this handsome gay man. His name was James, and he told Rhys that on first impression he thought Rhys was a good looking guy. I thought Rhys was going to stand up right there and do his happy dance in the isle of the oyster bar. It's unfortunate he didn't, because Rhys' happy dance makes everyone happy. This is validation for Rhys that could not be achieved from any other source. Generally speaking, gay men can be very particular about men's appearance. So receiving a compliment from one of them ranks high in Rhys' book of manliness.

As we strolled through the Castro district after dinner, Rhys was the object of many men's flirtatious attention. WOW! It's sort of surreal for me to be in an area as populated with gay men as the Castro District. All my life, I have been the object of unwanted attention by certain men who fail to recognize that extended stares equal sexual harassment. Rhys has his tail feathers ruffled on the occasions when I have been checked out by other men. Now here we are in a city with plenty of men, and not one is showing an ounce of interest in me! I think I love it! Women check Rhys out all the time, but now that he is fully immersed in his transition the gay men are on high alert! I think it will become increasingly interesting to see how much of the gay population will mistake Rhys as a gay man. The only reason this is entertaining to me and not threatening is because Rhys is as heterosexual a male as I would ever want to be in the company of. These wonderful gay men look at Rhys and then glance quickly to see who he is with, and then they give me the look of ignorant pity that says, "Do you realize you're with a gay man, Honey?!" Me, a fag hag. Beautiful. This could turn out to be hilarious. After Rhys no longer has boobs, we will have to put my theory to the test on the streets of San Francisco.

Later, lying in his comforting arms, I realized with a wave of sorrow that Rhys will no longer have sensation from his nipples after tonight. Loosing sensation in part of your body is a loss, but I've not talked to Rhys about it much. He may not feel it as a loss, but it's been devastating for me. I'm scared of all the things I am losing with every single one of his gains.

February 7, 2006

It's 4:30 in the morning and Rhys and I are wide awake lying together in each other's arms in the morning blackness. He is eerily calm, and I'm pretty sure that I could vomit on command. I try my damnedest to hide this disturbing fact from him. We discuss the looming day ahead, he feels ready to go forward. The surgery center is expecting us to arrive at 6:15 a.m. to register. Giving ourselves a lenient 45 minutes, hyper-prepared with MapQuest directions, we head out into the San Francisco darkness. After coming to a freeway onramp that has been detoured, we finally end up near our "supposed" destination. We had been driving around in an industrial area under a freeway overpass, with no luck at all. I rang the surgeon's cell to find out where to go.

Turns out we have the wrong directions.

FUCK ME!

My normally calm demeanor is quickly giving way to all the anxiety built up in my gut. Someone is going to cut open the beautiful, milky white flesh of my lover! Someone we haven't even met yet! Could this possibly be classified as a high stress factor situation? The San Francisco populous unwittingly helps guide us to our trans surgical destination, as we randomly stop to ask pedestrians for directions every block along the way.

We arrived at a medical office building just in time for Rhys to be registered and whisked away into the recesses of the surgery center. And there I stood alone, facing all the emotion welling up within me. There have been few moments in my life where I have felt as entirely alone as this one. The surgery center is a smorgasbord of sorts. Many people, many different types of doctors, a multitude of surgeries. Two women, one peacefully knitting, were obviously waiting for someone to come out of surgery. As I sat many people came in, quickly registered, and were called back to begin the pre-op process of surgery. After waiting for what seemed like a frickin' eternity, I was called back to visit Rhys as he was waiting in a pre-op room. He was already gowned with an IV trailed out of the back of his left hand.

"Look at my sexy socks," he sarcastically pointed out.

He was wearing white compression stockings up to his thighs. The staff at the center was exceptional and I felt so respected and confident in the care they were giving Rhys. The anesthesiologist came in and quizzed Rhys on his medical history. She then had a nurse inject a drug into his IV, which looped him out in a millisecond.

Everything happened so quickly. Before I had the opportunity to fall into an emotional heap, they came and took Rhys away on his gurney. With tears welling up and threatening to pour, I said goodbye to my lover. He looked back at me like a kid in line for a carnival ride, and replied with all the emotionless effect of his drug induced state,

"Bye"

That was it. Not one clue from him about what he was feeling whatsoever. I now believe it had to be this way for him to proceed.

The surgery took all of an hour and a half. Imagine that. Forty-one years of physical disassociation and ninety minutes to metamorphosis. During that time, I walked to the corner drugstore and filled Rhys' prescription for Percocet. I had every intention of keeping him as heavily sedated as possible. In the span of two blocks, I somehow misplaced my wallet. Great. I'm in San Francisco, Rhys is in surgery, and I can't find my only source of money, my only form of ID. So I turned back and sprinted the two blocks to the surgery waiting room to gratefully find my wallet lying on the floor next to the chair I had been sitting in. Just in time, too. The doctor came out to speak with me. I went into panic mode. *Something must have gone wrong. It's too soon for him to be out here.* My mind trailed off into unwarranted anxiety. He was actually there to tell me Rhys was doing great, and that he was very happy with the results of Rhys' surgery. The surgeon didn't show much emotion. But who cares? He just gave Rhys the best gift of his life—a flat chest.

After thirty minutes, I was led back to the recovery area to see Rhys. He was lying on a gurney with a pale face like the color of Elmer's glue. Pasty and butt-white. He was in his own happy/unhappy place, and couldn't say much. I bawled my eyes out. What a relief to be reunited finally and know the surgery was over. A nurse gave me instructions on how to care for Rhys—drainage tubes, chest binders, pain, medications and all—and then released us soon afterwards.

I got Rhys back home as quickly as possible. I had to park a block away—the streets of San Francisco are cruel—from our flat. Rhys, still affected by the anesthesia, somehow managed to amble from the rental car to the house—a journey that he has no memory of to this day. The whole experience was surreal. In the past, I could care for my children by picking them up and pulling them into the safety and the warmth of my own body. But all I could do for Rhys was find a way to get his clothes off, prepare a nest of sorts in the bed, and get him in as quickly and as comfortably as possible. He napped for about an hour.

When Rhys woke up, the first thing he wanted was food—a real meal.

"Chicken Parmesan would be really good for me right now," he said with confidence.

WRONG!

As quickly as he gobbled down the lunch, he offered it back up in the urgent form of steamy, overflowing, spaghetti vomit. I felt so horrible. I also completely hated him for a minute. I truly should have known better than to let him eat that kind of food so soon after surgery. After I cleaned up the bed, the floor, the bathroom, and Rhys—not necessarily in that order—he got back into bed and slept off and on for the remainder of the day while I stood a vigilant watch.

February 9, 2006

Rhys is doing amazingly well when considering the shock his body has just gone through. He is eating well (shocker), up, and watching movies. We have invented a system of propping bolsters underneath each arm to ease the stress and pain in his chest area. We walk and take drives along the ocean. The sunshine can't hurt in healing this winter weary Minnesotan. Over all, things are better than I anticipated. Rhys is wearing an elastic binder around his chest to protect and contain the tubes and sutures in his body. Who could have predicted that, with all the incisions he has underneath, it would be the actual binder itself that would cause him the worst pain and suffering of the entire experience. He began itching under the binder a few days ago, and that itching had grown to insanity in the last twenty-four hours.

Today, after going out on my own for a run, I returned to find Rhys in a state of anxiety, "Get this thing off me!!" he begged, as he tried to hitch-up the tight elastic band. I took the binder off and he wept tears of exasperation, "I am going insane with this itching, and I don't think I can take it anymore!!!" he exclaimed.

After doing my best possible job of propping him up, I walked to the nearest drugstore and bought some Gold Bond Powder to try and help relieve his pain and itching. When I got back, I found a much calmed trans boy. The powder made him smile, along with the nurse's uniform and red stilettos I secretly packed for the occasion. Nurse Ali saves the day.

February 13, 2006

Today is the first day that Rhys really feels well enough to be out in the world for a while. Good thing, because we have his first post-op visit to remove the annoying drains that are stitched into his oblique's. I have had the responsibility of emptying these bad boys three times a day. As the post-op time has grown, so has the thickness of the contents coming through the tubes. There were a few times that I held my impending gag until I made it to the bathroom and away from Rhys.

He wanted to buy a new shirt, a summer one. San Francisco has been blessedly sweet to us with her 75 degree temperatures. Rhys packed more winter shirts than summer ones, which cause him to sweat and itch under the restrictive binder. Wearing his new Castro-chic shirt, Rhys and I headed over to the doctor's office. The doctor pulled the tubes for what seemed like an eternity; they had to be at least twelve inches long! Sometimes, I have to just sit by and watch as Rhys goes through these ordeals. As the doctor was working, Rhys told the guy that he was in pain.

"This doesn't hurt." the doctor replied.

Rhys gave him a little bit of hell and rebutted, "It's my body, and if I say it hurts, then it hurts, OKAY?"

The guy just kind of chuckled and shook his head. Like I said before, bedside manner?!

From there, Rhys and I headed over to the wharf. We were feeling giddy about the next step of healing. The tubes were out, his chest was flat and he was wearing a spiffy new shirt. He was feeling great about himself and he looked the part.

They say timing is everything. We were in a store and a gay man approached Rhys and politely asked, "Can I help you find anything, *Ma'am*?"

Shit! SHIT!

I watched Rhys deflate and his stature shrink, as though he were the wicked witch of the west melting into the floor. Then retort, "Did you just call me *Ma'am*? Because I'm not a *MA'AM*! Give me a break! I'm sporting a brand new eight-thousand-dollar chest here!"

The man begged for Rhys' forgiveness, but Rhys turned and walked out of the store.

I have witnessed so much damage from one single word such as Ma'am. The problem is not so much what the man carelessly said, but how Rhys immediately began to question his own masculinity because of it. It is difficult for me to focus on my own feelings about this, because Rhys' feelings of anger and frustration filled the entire air space for a five mile radius. I felt helpless. Any meager offering of words or encouragement from me were futile as a squirt gun in a three alarm fire. Our afternoon of connectedness and fun immediately ended because of a stranger's ignorance around gender.

I can't help but wonder when this will ever end. Every time Rhys and I are in public, we subject ourselves to the likelihood of being misunderstood and even disrespected around his gender identity and our relationship. It puts a whole new spin on my willingness (or lack of it) to venture outside with Rhys. PTSD from this type of public interaction follows me each and every time we're out in the world and it is an unwanted companion to both of us.

Stealth is Rhys' dream right now.

February 14, 2006

We ventured out for an ocean drive this morning: me behind the wheel and Rhys sitting shotgun. We propped pillows under each of his arms to lessen the friction of the incisions. Unwittingly, we ended up driving up a winding hill that seemed more like a mountain range and made Rhys car sick and irritable as all hell. I had no idea where I was going, and between the winding roads and Rhys' rising level of frustration and pain, I had seen my better moments. Somehow though, I managed to get us back to our flat and put Rhys to bed for some much needed rest. My stress reduction therapy is running, so I strapped on my iPod and challenged the hills of San Francisco, taking a self-guided tour of the neighborhood.

It's difficult for me to care for myself while I'm caring for Rhys. There never feels like enough time for both of our needs. The self-care that usually brings me comfort is being pushed to the back burner. Yet I have become increasingly aware that if I don't take care of myself, my resentment toward his needs will inevitably build and I will become incapable of caring for him in his hours (and hours) of need. Caregiving is a slippery slope, as being a conscientious caregiver also requires a minimum level of self-care. Being with a transgender person in the midst of transitioning requires a strong commitment to both self and other. At times I feel guilty or selfish about a silent commitment I have made to myself. But in the same moment, I realize my self-denial could become unhealthy if taken to an extreme. Right now our lives seem to be about the story of this transition. It won't always be this way; I know this.

However, if I lose my "self" in the midst of Rhys finding himself, then I fear we won't be able to remember the place of love where we started.

February 15, 2006

Today is another milestone in Rhys' healing process; he gets the stitches in his chest taken out. I'm excited for each move toward his freedom, *our* freedom; yet, I'm hesitant about our impending return home tomorrow. The procedure to remove the sutures was flawless and a great relief to Rhys. His body is now free of any foreign medical matter remaining from the surgery. It is now his responsibility to do the rest of the work...HEAL.

February 16, 2006

This morning we packed our things with some hesitancy and headed back to frigid Minneapolis and, unfortunately, back to the reality of our everyday lives. We don't live together, and I'm not looking forward to the break in the depth of intimacy created by this surgical experience. Rhys seems to be improving every day. Most of all the chest binder and it's insane, persistent, itching, has been the worst post-op issue so far. I know that when we return, life will be difficult for Rhys once again. He will be under the scrutiny of everyone who knows he went to San Francisco to have chest surgery. Just imagine everyone looking at your chest, their eyes glued to your body and wondering what's going on underneath your shirt...Oh! Wait! That sounds vaguely familiar. Could it be because it's also been a version of my own reality as a cisgender woman for the past twenty-five years? I'm anxious to see how Rhys will deal with people's consistent curiosity.

We left San Francisco and its unseasonable seventy degree temperatures to arrive in Minneapolis at thirty below with wind chills. A negative one hundred degree difference! Not the homecoming I would have liked. At the moment, Rhys and I are living in separate houses, but only four miles apart. Today however, those four miles seem like distant continents. After the intense experience we just went through, it seems preposterous for me to drop him off and venture home by myself. I'm worried at the thought of it, and so is Rhys. This is our reality at the moment. We've never discussed cohabiting before, and even in his acute state, neither he nor I have dared to venture down that road. I'm nervous to jump into moving in. My independence has become my crutch, and I'm not sure what it will take to put it down. Maybe Rhys' need for a caregiver isn't the best reason?

February 19, 2006

Rhys is reaching his limit of patience with how long his recovery is taking. And perhaps I, too, have arrived at mine. We are both physically exhausted and have functioned on less than eight hours of sleep every night for the past ten nights. My head feels numb and I feel like my response to life in general is skewed. Coming back to our customary lives has not proven to be an easy transition for either of us. Since we don't live together...well, this single point is proving to be the most physically and emotionally taxing piece for both of us. Daily, I'm driving over to his place to help him change the dressings on his incisions and apply anti-itch lotion on the affected areas underneath the binder. His healing is going surprisingly well. Nonetheless,

Rhys comments several times a day that some part of his new chest doesn't look right. I can feel the fear in his comments that perhaps his chest won't turn out the way he thought it would. And now, here we are thousands of miles—and one hundred stinkin' degrees!—away from the doctor who performed his surgery. It's altogether possible I don't care, because personally I think the doctor's "bedside manner" could use some major fine tuning. Rhys argues that it's not important, since he is reportedly the best at what he does in the whole damn country. Wanting the doctor to acknowledge that this procedure was conceivably the biggest decision Rhys has made in his entire life was perhaps too big a request. Each day, I deal with Rhys' frustrations and his growing level of impatience with a sickeningly sweet amount of positive reinforcement. And he knows damn well that I'm pouring it on, but takes my gift of altruism with no rebuttal. Perhaps it's what he needs to get him to heal completely. I often wonder how long we will be able to carry on living in two separate places during this time of incredible need for physical and emotional intimacy. I gently asked Rhys to promise me that he won't plan anymore surgeries until we are living together. He wholly agreed.

CHAPTER 3

A First Time For Everything

~

February 20, 2006

RHYS WENT TO A MEN'S ROOM for the first time today. We were having lunch at our favorite Greek restaurant when nature called. This time, however, it wasn't met by the urgency to leave and race back home so he could relieve himself. Instead, he quietly informed me of his bold new plan, got up before I had a chance to complain, and entered the men's room. There, at our table, I was left with myself and my growing feelings of lack of control and protectiveness all rolled together in one wad. I watched the bathroom door like a hawk to make sure no other men entered while Rhys was in there. What I thought I would do if a guy *did* go in, I didn't have a clue. In that moment, my mind flashed to horrific scenes from the movie, *Boys Don't Cry*, and I feared for Rhys' life over something as simple as taking a leak. The moments I waited seemed to stand still, each for itself, and it felt like he was in there for eternity. What could I do if he were gone too long in a men's room? If I raced in and found him in the stall doing his business, I would be met by turned heads at the urinals and an escort back out the door into the real world.

Bathrooms are a big part of his process right now. I never imagined this part a year ago. Rhys and I have become hyper-conscious of the places in our city that offer gender-neutral bathrooms, and they have earned our loyal patronage. Some of these places offer substandard food quality and dining experiences, but I don't care because it means he can get up and pee whenever he needs. Such is the world we live in, where bathroom safety and availability takes precedence over an organic, vegan menu choice. Much to my relief he exited from his maiden voyage unscathed with his chest out and a huge grin on his face.

"*I did it.*" he leaned in and whispered.

"How was it?" I questioned.

"Disgusting!" he exclaimed, "Turns out men really are pigs!"

Thank whoever for the humor we find in this process.

February 22, 2006

As Rhys' body improves, his spirits seem to plummet. I don't know what the fuck to do. I'm so damn tired, and I keep trying to find something more to give. Something to get him, to get us, through this hard time. I realize in hindsight it would have been valuable to have had some more time off after returning home from San Francisco. We both feel too vulnerable to be in public. We are the "IT" couple right now. And "IT" sucks. Everyone wants to talk about Rhys, to Rhys, about his body. Don't get me wrong. People are concerned and supportive, and it's great to know that we have a community. But at the moment, it's a double-edged scalpel (Oops! Did I just say that out loud?), having just returned from one of the rawest experiences I've ever had. Rhys doesn't want to be the topic of discussion anymore.

He summarizes with such beautiful simplicity his entire life's goal:

"I just want to *pass.*"

And to compound his frustration, Rhys and I haven't been able to be intimate in the normal fashion we are fond of and accustomed to. To be apart from each other when we need nothing greater than to be close is creating a rift that I could never have anticipated. We are only three months in, and I'm already fried from the process of transition. I want Rhys. Right here, right now, just exactly the way he is. I don't need another whisker, or a deeper resonance in his voice. In the words of Billy Joel, Rhys, "I want you just the way you are."

I don't know how to convey the depth of my love to him right now without hurting him. He wants to change, and I know that change will bring about more and more peace and self-confidence. So if I say how I am happy with where he is right now in the transition I may give him the impression that I don't want him to change anymore. But if I tell him that I can't wait for all his changing to be done, then he could have the false impression that I am discontent with where he is at the moment. Screwed!—with a capital S. This is a road less traveled. Perhaps even a road *not* traveled? Tomorrow is a new day, and everyday an opportunity to love him right where he stands. Yet, I'm often unsure if I'm up to the task.

This morning, a careless, uninformed, yet, well-meaning clerk *"Ma'am-ed"* Rhys. If one more person calls my boyfriend-lover-transman *"Ma'am,"* I think my violent alter ego will burst through. The thing is this: Don't call people "MA'AM," period! Not anyone. Not ever.

Not Rhys.

Not even me.

These labels are so insidiously patronizing and archaic. It would probably be safer to err on the side of sir. Anyone? Can you help me out here? If you were in the face of someone who has a tendency towards androgyny, would you take a stab at it and call them *MA'AM?* No, you wouldn't (Or you shouldn't). We in the non-trans (cis-gendered) world, take for granted every day and in every situation, that we will be seen and recognized as the gender we present. It would only take a handful of the horrifying accounts of public humiliation that Rhys has endured on a daily basis to send the average person running back into their house and locking the doors.

February 23, 2006

If we moved far, far away, and started over, then Rhys could be the man he is with no questions asked. The anonymity of our situation would be the ticket to his gender freedom. I've been thinking quite a bit about on how Rhys is physically transforming in front of an audience of his peers. There's no way for him to hide. Each new whisker, each surgery, and his ever-deepening voice is there, front and center for all of society to view and critique. On the whole, people mean well. They want to show their support even through their confusion and discomfort. I have a new appreciation for the process of puberty. My son (at the hormonal pinball age of 16) is changing before my eyes, and I am suddenly aware of how uncomfortable this process must be for every teenager in the world because Rhys is in puberty as well.

Everyone is analyzing his daily physical process. So acquaintances will comment, "Wow! Your voice is so deep; I didn't even recognize you!"

A bit of an overkill at this stage.

Moments like these I feel like I'm on the outside looking in, and it feels a little voyeuristic. I can only sit back and watch as he maneuvers his way through this thirty year delayed puberty.

February 25, 2006

Last night for my birthday, Rhys took me to a great restaurant that's owned and frequented by LGBTQ people—a place where I can let my breath out and just be with my trans boyfriend. He looked so hot when he first stepped out of the front door; he made me go all weak in the knees! His black turtleneck now hugs the line of his new defined pecs. He had on a brown dinner jacket and a pair of Lucky jeans. How apropos because I was feeling just that lucky.

Our dinner was wonderful: great food, elegant, intimate atmosphere despite the gay man at the bar checking Rhys out as often as possible. We were not paid attention to by anyone but the staff, and that's where things went sour. Just when I dared venture to that place where the evening had been nothing short of perfect, our ever-so-effeminate gay waiter came over to our table and asked, "Would you *ladies* like to have dessert?"

Ladies!

DEVASTATION! Thanks for nothing motherfucker, you just ruined my birthday. Is this a trend with the gay men, or just my overactive imagination? From what I can tell, gay men calling each other ladies is about the equivalent of women friends calling each other bitch. It's accepted on most levels and it even goes so far as to be a term of endearment. I immediately corrected our queenie waiter. He was so undone by the foot in his mouth that he had to wait a few seconds before listing what was on the dessert menu. Chocolate mousse cake sounds a lot less appealing after being grossly insulted. Rhys said it was okay, and that he was fine. But I could tell by the speediness at which we made our exit that the full truth of his emotions had not yet been revealed.

After getting into the truck, Rhys began to self-analyze what feminine part of him could possibly have been the rationale behind the waiter's comment. It's like trying to explain color to a blind person. Who knows where this waiter has been in his life and what brought him to this moment, this perception of Rhys? It's never the right time after these linguistic gauntlets have fallen on Rhys to explain to him what I am beginning to realize about this prevalent situation in our lives. But here it is: If he continues to allow other people's perception of him to determine his own self-image and self-worth then he won't progress in this transition. Everyone has their own perception of everything they experience. When these mistaken references are made, I am always taken aback. Perhaps people wonder why I feel this way. After all, I *am* dating a "female-to-male" transgender person. But that's the amazing thing about perception; no two people experience the same event in the same way, ever. There is no completely objective appraisal of anything. No wonder when a car accident occurs that the drivers of the vehicles involved sound like they have been driving on opposite ends of the city, instead of being intimately attached to their own vehicles. The mind is a powerful thing and changes its perception constantly. The only perception I claim to feel definite about is my own. Everything about Rhys to me is masculine. I can't find a feature on his face that appears feminine. His gestures are masculine, his voice is masculine, and his hair and face are those of a man. Rhys' energy creates the reality of my perception of him. In turn, my energy returned to him reinforces his masculinity. This is the way we live in our day-to-day lives together. To be out in the public eye and have people perceive Rhys as feminine is no less than shocking to me. While he is learning to be more accepting of these verbal faux pas, I am feeling increasingly defeated. Perhaps it's because no one else is privy to the emotional pain that Rhys constantly experiences, and at some level they don't have the base level of consciousness to see who he really is. I can only hope that as his process of masculinization occurs, these gender errors will become a thing of the past for both of us. Wrapping my brain around this part is emotionally painful and exhausting. Good thing it was my 42nd birthday and not my 24th because I never would have had the stamina, or the maturity, to deal with people and their comments the way I am able to now.

March 2, 2006

I'm blown away at the depths to which my relationship with Rhys has taken me. For the first time in my life, I am learning what the word intimacy truly is. I'm not talking sex here; that part is like a rampant storm that takes us both without warning and without ceasing until its energy is fully spent. No, I mean the kind of opening of the soul to another person that allows you to see deeper into yourself through your own reflection shining in their eyes. It will possibly qualify (and triumph), as the riskiest behavior I have ever involved myself in. Perhaps the discovery of self is only fully possible through being vulnerable to another person.

We are dancing together this beautiful, delicate dance that requires profound concentration and consciousness. One misstep and we lose our footing and step all over each other. Perhaps this deserves a more detailed and in-depth explanation.

For all of my adult life, I have played the roles of mother and homemaker, until I awoke one day from my sleepwalking state of invalidation. After 20 years in a relationship with a man who became too predictable during for the last 10, I realized with lightning clarity that it was past time for me to move on. During that period, however, I was a servant to family: my family. It is such a powerfully humble act to be a stay-at-home mom, financially dependent on another person. In a perfect world this setup could work beautifully. The partner whose majority of time was spent on financially providing for the family would have the utmost respect and awe for the partner whose majority of time was spent on maintaining a beautiful, well-run home and devotion to the needs of any children they may have.

In my relationship, my contribution was undervalued by my spouse simply because my work was not paid work. Whatever his perception, I personally found my tasks deeply grounding and gratifying at the end of each day. But as time passed, my resentment toward my spouse greatly outgrew my own ability to find self-fulfillment in being home. Pity, because I truly felt I was doing my life's work at that time more than ever before, or since.

Fast forward five years. Here I am, sitting in my *own* home, owning my *own* small business which I built myself, and having a sudden enlightenment that is at times unnerving. As I open myself deeper and deeper to the intimacy that is offered before me every day with Rhys, I realize that I am yearning to make a home for him and me together. Just when I thought that "having it all" would fill the void within me I'm also becoming aware of what I really desire for myself. Since the day I first spoke to Rhys, he has validated every word I have shared.

It's not the dance itself that makes our relationship work, but the beautiful way that Rhys executes his every step around my feminine mystique. I yearn for the two of us to make a family of our own and to share in the beautiful, mundane intimacy of living in the same house. I want to wake up to his adorable face, and to see his toothbrush drying on the back of the sink. Being a part of the experience of his transition, I feel that if I miss one moment, I miss volumes of his experience. *Our* experience.

My fear of physical distance in our living separately has grown into a fear of losing emotional connection with him. Up to this point, we haven't talked much about living together. My youngest child is still a minor and this alone keeps Rhys and I geographically separate. Yet, eventually I know something will need to change. It has to. He and I can't attempt to pretend the way we are living is a long term solution. The million-dollar question is who will be the first to breech the subject? Rhys is the one with the beautiful two-story house. I can't imagine a scenario where he would leave his place to move in with me. My place is only 750 square feet, and while it's cute, it could never house his personality. So for now we are at a silent impasse, and I intend to leave it that way. As much as I fantasize about a life living with Rhys, I'm not willing to risk bringing it up.

March 6, 2006

Something emotionally is going on with Rhys. But *he* doesn't know what's going on, which leaves me in the dark. I didn't see him for more than ten minutes today, and it's painful how empty I feel inside. Void. As hard as this transition has been at times my life feels like the sum of these moments. There is an urgency and intensity to our lives in and around his transition. Not seeing him for a day is like missing out on a piece of the story. I ache for him. He grounds me, and yet, he makes me feel fucking crazy. It's extremely difficult at times to have the insight on how to approach his mood. Sometimes saying nothing is best. When I deviate from my intuition, I end up saying a lot that ends up feeling like nothing.

I know he has situational depression. He says it's not because of the current changes, but because of what he cannot—will never—be able to change. He has a deep feeling of grief in his current situation. It's complicated and messy. And then there is me, wanting him to be emotionally vulnerable when often he can't even identify his emotional state for himself. Being with Rhys when he is suffering from depression is like calling through the fog and getting no reply. A different persona is present. His body looks heavier, his face darker, and his eyes are like dark pools of pain. I am challenged to remain connected to Rhys, and simultaneously take care of myself.

So I do what I can for Rhys—cook a meal, rub his feet, touch his face as he leaves—and hope that these actions will love him back into himself.

We go out less often now than ever before. Rhys has subconsciously decided he is much more content to be at home. I see a change in his attitude about his transition, too. Instead of expecting to transform overnight into a GQ cover model—which is the direction he's headed—he is starting to accept and settle into the idea this could be a slower, yet sometimes wild ride.

The stress of his frustration can make any situation almost unbearable for me. He is still frustrated, but there is no mistaking the very apparent physical changes he is acquiring. Facial widening, a more evident beard, darker body hair, and a voice that deepens so quickly he gets asked if he is getting over a cold. Crazy to think that just three months ago he was physically recognized as female. Since that time he has entered into a place of limbo, teetering on the side of a fully masculinized body. Not fast enough for Rhys, but if it happened any quicker there would need to be an owner's manual of some sort.

I'm having difficulty running at the pace that his changes require. No longer am I seen as a lesbian. This was a short-lived categorization used by others to put me in a category that explained why I wasn't attracted to the average heterosexual cisgender male. But now I realize with incredible clarity that I am attracted to people who are genderqueer and that's merely one qualifying piece of my orientation. I feel no need at this point for a label to go with that statement, but society appears to demand just that. It has me wondering exactly how many people are walking around every day feeling like they have been required to live in a sexual identity prison by not fitting into our archaic binary gender system. The people in my life who really matter to me need no further explanation of my choices beyond loving Rhys.

March 10, 2006

My boyfriend has become an exhibitionist. At any given moment, he is prone to ask, "You wanna see my nipples?" Before a response can be formulated in my brain, he whips up his shirt and proudly displays his newly sculpted pec muscles. I am so damn relieved that he is pleased with the results of his surgery. I think all along I've worried a little that he may come out of the whole experience unhappy with how he looks. And twelve thousand dollars later, that would be a major bummer! Rhys looks incredible. Not only does he have a new chest, but his chest area is widening. He stands up straighter, shoulders back, chin up. I'm dating a peacock.

He is increasingly confident in his new emerging physique. Before surgery, Rhys would roll his shoulders forward to hide the telltale evidence of his female body. By doing so, his shirt would hang out from his chest, hiding the fact that he had boobs. Every morning he had to carefully navigate the closet to find the outfit that looked the most masculine. If a shirt had the slightest cling to his body it was thrown aside. His tendency was toward clothing that was far too large for his form. His favorite clothing stores were often off limits due to their tailored clothing. But not anymore! It has just come to my attention that the cost for this part of the transition has not been realized until the new wardrobe has been purchased. I can't think of anyone more deserving of a shopping spree than a trans man sporting a new chest! Banana Republic, meet Rhys!!!

March 13, 2006

Minneapolis. Twelve inches of snow and no way out. That means no trans lovin' today. I'm so sick of living in separate houses. Something inside Rhys appears to be distancing him from the entire world, including me. We're having a hard time understanding each other lately. It remains extremely difficult to attempt an emotional connection over the phone.

March 18, 2006

Before Rhys' transitioning began, he had a personal hygiene regimen that teetered on an Obsessive Compulsive Disorder. Haircuts, clothing, cologne, lint brushes, belts, shoes; all of it was part of his everyday morning routine. He is often mistaken for a gay man, and, forgive my generalization, but in large part because of the stylish, impeccable way he dresses. Then, enter testosterone. Not only are there daily physical changes, but there are peeks of changes in Rhys' previous obsessive style. I'm noticing less hair product and more jeans. It's curious and cute all wrapped into one trans guy. As these changes mildly progress, it leaves me guessing where this will take us. He is changing right before my eyes, more than he even realizes. I am noticing a growing thickness to his upper torso, and when I am in his embrace I feel fully enveloped by him. Just yesterday, I became aware that his hands and fingers are broadening. He appears to be literally bursting out of his flesh. This week he was addressed as "Sir" many times, thank you. He still prefers hanging out at home, but when we are out, not being called "*Ma'am*" is a welcome relief to him. I've begun to realize that soon Rhys will be perceived as male to everyone in public.

Finally!

Because of the gradual and sometimes painful pace of this process, it seems that he doesn't realize the dramatic nature of his changes. Soon he will have no option but to use the men's bathroom. He mentions to me that he isn't ready to graduate into that yet. *God protect him when he is*! As a woman, I haven't a clue what goes on in a room where men all piss in each other's presence, and it's a cluelessness I intend to hold on to.

March 21, 2006

Returning from his therapy appointment today, Rhys shared with me some of the conversation that went on behind closed doors. His therapist bluntly inquired, "So what attracts Ali to transgender men?"

Simple enough. Let me see here. I know that if I recede into the smoke screen of my childhood, I can recall always being intrigued by those who were called tomboys. I know also that I didn't have the insight then, or in the twenty-five years following, to realize a defined "attraction." In my thirties, I began to seek out and befriend many lesbians. It was through those relationships that I was included in many social gatherings and parties where women of varying sexual orientations were present. I was rarely physically or sexually attracted to the women who proudly claimed the title of lesbian. But I do remember one party in the suburb where I lived—yes, there really are lesbians living in the suburbs! —where a person was present with his/her partner. I am not sure what this person identified as. I never had the opportunity to speak to him/her in person. But what I believe now based on my introduction into the world of gender fluidity, is that this person was a transgender man. They had a cropped haircut, and wore small, scholarly looking glasses. Their clothing style was intellectual, bookish: freshly creased khakis with an argyle sweater. And either they were binding—using tight elastic binders to hide breasts—or successfully hunched over enough to hide any physical characteristics of a female chest. The person didn't intermingle with the women at the party, and after observing this particular lesbian community, I would see why. The women were talking about their menstrual cycles, and what size yoga pants they buy…for real! As a trans man, Rhys says the group he believes is most uncomfortable with his transition is the lesbian community.

As I've watched Rhys through this process, it's become apparent to me that some people in the lesbian "community" (and I use this term loosely) are personally offended, even threatened, by him becoming physically what he has always felt his gender to be. It would appear in the eyes of some lesbians that Rhys is a "sellout." More than a few women who identify themselves as lesbians have said to me that "becoming" male is not respecting the lesbian community. But here's the thing, Rhys never really was a lesbian. He just hung out with them because it was the closest he could get to a safe place in our land of crumbling human rights.

I had multiple opportunities at the party to observe this person, and I would bet my thigh highs that this was a trans man. Perhaps he didn't even know it himself at the time; maybe he still doesn't. Hell, Rhys has only recently been introduced to the possibility of something outside of lesbianism. Many people have never even heard of the term "transgender," including those who would identify most comfortably in that community. So here stood this person, looking like they were about to crawl out of their own skin. And I know now, that I was drawn to him. Not just physically, but also out of curiosity. He was different and I was intrigued.

Flash forward a few years to a room where I was sitting with a group of people. In walked Rhys, and my body turned to him like the black-and-white magnetic toy Scottie dogs I had as a child. No matter which way the one was turned, the other was instantly attracted. There was an energy around him that was electrostatic. Is this because he is a trans person, or simply because he is Rhys? Can that question truly be answered? Because if so, it would have to turn something with intangible simplicity into a tangible complication.

Banana Republic, three o'clock on a Tuesday afternoon. Rhys and I are checking out the new spring duds and trying to be as incognito as possible. I walked away to try on a blouse and Rhys continued shopping in the men's area. When I came out unsuccessful, he was anxiously waiting for me. He grabbed my hand and whispered, "Come on, let's go!"

Immediately, I began to imagine what gender identity atrocities had transpired in the few short minutes I had spent in the dressing room. Sweet Mother of All Things Good and Trans, I was wrong! Rhys could barely contain himself. As we exited his favorite place for retail therapy, he began to recount for me how many times the male clerk had addressed him as "sir."

"Can I help you find anything, *Sir*?"

"How are you today, *Sir*?"

"Is there a size that I can get for you, *Sir*?"

Rhys was so happy, I thought he was going to bust open from being addressed as a guy. As he recounted their exchange, Rhys started to see himself as the man at Banana Republic saw him. He began to perceive himself as having a fully transitioned male appearance. This is the exact opposite of what happens when someone addresses him with a female pronoun. The self-examination that takes place after those misnomers include an exhaustive and self-critical search of how he continues to inadvertently project any measure of femininity: constantly checking himself in the rearview mirror to try and see what everyone else sees. Regardless of how much self-confidence we have, the way others perceive us has an enormous impact on how we feel and think about ourselves. So today Rhys was perceived as male by a complete stranger, and the remainder of the day he stayed in the energy of that recognition.

As time passes and Rhys adds to his five o'clock shadow, he is gradually becoming what is identified by our society as "male." I say this because no matter what, Rhys will always have been born transgender. Eventually, he will walk in the world as a man. I see his transformation is quickly progressing, but Rhys has a difficult time staying in that belief when others misperceive him.

We went to the court building downtown to pick up forms to change Rhys' legal name and gender. We asked about changing his birth certificate, too. The process is a lot of legal red tape. Once his name and gender are legally male, he won't hesitate to show his driver's license or credit card. Between the chest reconstruction, the quickly changing facial appearance and the pending name change, Rhys is on the verge of becoming legally male (not to be confused with legally blonde!). The possibilities that this creates are encouraging. I no longer qualify him as anything but my boyfriend when talking to a new person. I won't divulge the vulnerable underbelly of our true relationship to society at large, not because I lack pride in being part of the LGBTQ community, but because of my fierce protectiveness of Rhys, his body and precious soul.

March 29, 2006

Doctor appointment today. Not so good news about getting the next surgical procedure paid by health insurance. Apparently, even if he had health insurance (which let me add, is a crisis among self-employed people due to the out-of-pocket costs), the procedure of removing his unwanted internal organs would be considered an elective "transgender" procedure. So that leaves Rhys yet again with the financial responsibility of a major surgery. This time the expense would be twelve thousand dollars. Now can someone answer me this: Who the hell has that kind of money? If a child was born without a limb, would the medical community place the entire financial responsibility of a prosthetic on the family?

Recently I watched a riveting documentary called "Emmanuel's Gift." It is a film exposing the little known fact that in Ghana, South Africa, twenty percent of the population is born with some type of physical birth defect. The culture believes that these people with disfigured bodies are aberrations, and they are cast out and looked upon as a curse on their family. They are forced to become beggars on the street. Can any society (such as our very own) that looks down upon people born into a physical body that is incongruent with their soul, be any more civilized than that in Ghana? Who are we trying to fool here in America, hiding behind archaic religious traditions and beliefs? I have been told throughout my life that I ask far too many questions. But the truth is I have barely even begun to ask.

The film explained that Ghana is moving towards education and ultimately changing against this ancient belief. In this country, land of the free and home of the brave, we appear to be moving rapidly in the opposite direction.

God help us.

The second tidbit of information that the doctor informed us of today is that the next procedure for reconstruction Rhys has been considering (genital surgery), may not have the physical outcome he had hoped for. It requires three separate surgeries all performed in Arizona, months of recovery time, and approximately sixty thousand dollars. Cash. And that is just for the procedure. Watching for Rhys' response out of the corner of my eye, I noticed he didn't flinch upon hearing this news.

On a more positive note, according to the doctor he is progressing nicely in his transition. He got a prescription to refill the magical testosterone, which I've renamed the love serum. Rhys currently has the sexual appetite and stamina of ten people. And he definitely wasn't in any need of the other nine joining in. I'm thinking maybe I should begin doubling my daily dose of estrogen so I can keep up. Then again, maybe I don't need to.

As Rhys becomes ever more at home in his dream body, he emits an energy that is undeniable to the average passing woman. I have personally witnessed women going out of their way just to walk in his path. Most of the time, they're non-threatening for me. But the other day, I tagged along with Rhys to his anatomy class. While he was teaching, a female student (who previously shared with Rhys her attraction to trans men), casually invited him to take a class with her in California for three weeks. *Hmmm*, could this be interpreted as more than just a quest for increased knowledge, or am I slightly paranoid?

I refuse to become the jealous girlfriend, but it is interesting to note how women perceive Rhys. The boundaries become blurred when they are in his presence, and I watch as otherwise professional, intelligent, women turn into giggling, flirting young girls. Wow, it takes a strong sense of self and confidence to be with someone who is receiving so much uninvited, amorous attention. If the situation were reversed (and at times it has been), I'd see one badass, territorial, trans boy. It's fine though, because I know who he loves and respects. But just an aside: Women, back down or I'll kick your flirtatious asses!

March 30, 2006

Today in a conversation with Rhys he suggested the LGBTQ community (as it presently stands), should really be changed to the G/L community. The lesbians continue to wage their battle on his transformation. Nearly every one of the women we know in the lesbian community has been resistant to Rhys' request to be identified as male. He appears to be a threat to what they believe about themselves. I'm not sure why this is, but my guess would be that he challenges them to look at their own places of masculinity just by being truthful about his transition. And perhaps that is a place they have never explored in themselves.

I interviewed a new therapist today. Since my insightful and confrontational therapist retired at the ripe young age of 48, I struggle to find a place where once I bring up the topic of my trans boyfriend, the focus still stays on me. I know Rhys' feathers are a brighter, more interesting color right now, but mine are in dire need of grooming. Keeping up with all Rhys' changes and being accountable to myself at the same time, has become a tall order.

Three years ago I began a process of consciously removing the smoke screens of my childhood that have kept me from knowing my own truths. In the midst of this, I discontinued all contact with my mother. Self-preservation at this point. Rhys has been the greatest support through my painful process, and his validation of my pain has been a main ingredient in my recipe for wholeness. I have cried so much that the skin under my eyes has become chapped and peeling from the salty tears. My closest friend has listened to unending hours of my ancient pain surfacing. She has made no judgments, only validation. These two people have loved me back to myself over the past three years. Words cannot express the depth of my gratitude. But now I need more guidance than just a listening ear. I sense an impending feeling of loss creeping in like winter's cold. Hopefully, I can find a place where my relationship with Rhys doesn't constantly upstage my own process.

April 2, 2006

Rhys' ability to transition goes beyond courageous and crosses into the realm of the unexplainable. Consider this: When I met Rhys he inhabited a female body, and loosely identified himself as a lesbian. Except for me, no one knew the inner struggle and discontent he experienced with his physical body. He inhabited that body, and filled it with the charming, dynamic energy that is the very fiber of his spirit. As he came to understand and acknowledge that he is transgender, he somehow made room for his transition. Now he is transitioning, and that exact same soul has found its home within his transforming body.

The resilience of the people I have met who make the decision to physically transition is truly inspiring. It isn't the knowledge of what they will face that is hard. It's not knowing and doing it anyway.

April 6, 2006

Today, Rhys called "Out Front," a Minnesota LGBTQ advocacy organization for information on the legal aspects of changing his name and gender. They knew nothing about the process! Go figure? So far, we are batting zero on the legal gender change. Our visit to the county courthouse was frustrating as well. Their system offers free legal advice, where you take a number and wait in plastic chairs along with the other marginalized and overlooked people in the waiting room. I'm an extremely tenacious person and am not easily deterred. However, if the advocacy groups assisting the LGBTQ community don't have the right information, then who the hell does? It appears that the legal issues for transgender individuals are too new to have a protocol. Next week, we'll come back and pursue it again downtown at the courthouse. We got nowhere today.

Rhys has now transitioned to a point where he is no longer mistaken for female. In trans lingo, the term is "stealth." Even beyond that, he has been curiously welcomed into the secret and elite society of "The Male." His observation of the disparity of respect between males and females is shocking. Rhys, who has been socialized and externally identified as a female for 42 years, is reentering the world as a man. As with all these examples, the insight that is gained by me is beyond amazing and moves toward shocking. When we are out together, Rhys gets a male "nod of approval" for who he is with. Seems the good ol' boys actually do have a code, a simple nod for "your woman is hot." Men are less likely to disrespect Rhys and me with inappropriate stares now. I'm learning that there is a level of respect between men regarding their female partners, which many men don't extend to women couples, as if the female-to-female relationship somehow has less (or no) validity.

As Rhys transitions, I too am transforming. Since society at large started to perceive Rhys as male, I have moved up a few notches on the cultural and patriarchal "respect-o-meter." Previously seen as a lesbian couple, we were often stared at and many times with disdain. Perceived as a man and woman, however, we are admired now. Immediate privilege. Yet, a part of me really grieves the loss of identification and acknowledgement within the LGBTQ community.

Rhys will soon be identified as male to everyone except those who knew about his previous process of transition. He is a transgender individual and his journey through that process is his greatest distinction, a beautiful attribute. However, most of the world will never know that part of him. If we show up at the LGBTQ Pride Festival this summer we'll look like one of those nice, evolved suburban couples who support diversity, possibly with great financial contributions, as a tribute to their recently outed college-age son…"GO GAYS!"

Somehow, this transition has become an oxymoron of sorts. Rhys both wants to pass as male and at the same time be validated as transgender. However, once he fully passes, he will no longer be identifiable as trans. The fulfillment of one wish will mean the death of the other. Another aspect of transitioning has become apparent to me: A trans person might forever live incongruent in their bodies. Rhys asked me how I would feel if I had the physical ache to be sexually intimate with someone but couldn't because I didn't have a vagina.

"How do you think *you* would feel?" he asked.

My answer was probably not even close to what he was hoping for. I explained to him that it would be an outright lie for me to say how I think that would feel. Because every minute of every day I occupy my female body and fill it with my feminine spirit. It isn't something that I spend too much time thinking about.

Those of us who feel that our biological sex matches our gender most likely take for granted, without even knowing it the peace that comes with that gift. This is what privilege feels like. After being with Rhys, I can never claim to know what it is like to be a transgender person. I tried to explain to him that I don't quite grasp what he is asking, not knowing anything other than what I have experienced in my own body. My female sense of self is congruent with my body. And for those whose bodies do not align with their spirits, they are mistaken in thinking that the rest of us could even remotely begin to understand their pain. I have learned how important it is to acknowledge the other person's experience. It bridges the gap between what I know for myself, and what Rhys tells me about his own experience. My understanding lies in my ability to empathize with the agony that I see and hear in Rhys every day.

April 7, 2006

Locally, there is a newspaper publication that serves the female population, The Minnesota Women's Press. I casually pick it up on my way out of the gym when it catches my eye. And today it caught more than that. "Transgender Among Us" read the headline in bold letters with a picture of a handsome young man in a baseball cap next to it. I couldn't wait to get to my car and read! The article described the discrimination that the man suffered as a preoperative transgender guy on the Minneapolis police force. He was given the option to use the women's restroom to pee, or not pee at all during his shift. He opted for the latter. Daily, he endured brutal harassment. He sued the police department for discrimination but lost and resigned soon after. Most trans identified people have suffered some form of blatant discrimination in their lives. I'm grateful for this article and its progressive take on the discrimination transgender people in Minneapolis face. Seeing more press and media attention given to the transgender community gives me great hope that Rhys and I will eventually find our niche someday.

April 9, 2006

Today we visited a couple of women (whose names have been changed here) who were Rhys' friends before I came into his life. They are wonderfully accepting and loving people, and I felt a bond with them in our first introduction last fall. Rhys has a close relationship with Lisa and they've hung out a few times since he had his surgery. But we have not seen Lisa's partner, Tammy, since before that time. Right away, Tammy asked Rhys if she could touch his chest. He didn't need to be begged to peel off his layers of clothing and proudly display his beautiful new chest. (Lately, he does this posing thing.... He flexes his arms forward and makes a grunting noise...*can I get a witness here?*) She was so excited to see how amazing he looked; I could tell immediately how important her opinion was to Rhys.

The four of us got into a lengthy and intimate conversation about his transition and my role as his partner/supporter. There were some terrific insights offered by these friends. Ultimately, I ended up in tears. I wasn't sad; my reaction was much more complex than that. This is the first time that Rhys and I have shared the vulnerability of our experience with anyone. As I heard Rhys expressing his thoughts and feelings, I was able to observe his process from a third person perspective. His words began to soak into my mind, then my body, they touched the deepest place in my heart.

I love this man.

His struggle and search for wholeness is possibly the most beautiful process I have been close to. Even when we're in a room filled with other people, I still feel deeply connected to him. It doesn't matter if he is sitting in the chair furthest from me our emotional bond bridges the gaps.

Tammy, Lisa and Rhys are many years sober and familiar with the twelve steps of Alcoholics Anonymous. Tammy suggested to Rhys that perhaps he could use some of the AA philosophies to get him through this period of in-between-ness. She reminded him that when you are a newly sober person, it is hard to believe or imagine a time will come when your every thought will not revolve around alcohol and staying sober. She went on to suggest that this process of transitioning could possibly be similar. Each day Rhys thinks about whether or not he continues to change physically, and whether or not society perceives him as male. Tammy thought maybe the comparison could help him to remember that now he has nearly ten years of sobriety he doesn't have to think about it in his every waking moment. In other words, his change is new and happening slowly, but there will come a day when this process will be over (for the most part), and Rhys will be living without the burden of these thoughts. What an insightful observation! What I find valuable are the perceptions of other people who Rhys trusts. Many of the thoughts and feelings I have shared with him are not taken the same way they would be if spoken by a close friend. At times, my place in Rhys' life proves to be too close when it comes to unbiased observation. I'm grateful that he's opening up to Lisa and Tammy; it helps distribute the weight of this transition to more people, and each of us can carry a small piece.

April 12, 2006

The raw and beautiful honesty of a child can sometimes replace my apathy for humankind with blinding hope. This afternoon, one of my clients (and Rhys' patient), had an appointment with me to get a massage. Unable to find child care, she brought along her four-year-old daughter. The preschooler sat in a chair in my studio and colored with her crayons while her mom relaxed on my massage table. When the massage was over, the little girl approached me with her angelic innocence, "But, um, I have one problem that I need to talk about Dr. Rhys." she began.

Her twisted brow and confused face showed that she was in deep, reflective thought. She continued, "How does he know for sure in his heart that he is a boy and that he is in the wrong body?"

Her mom obviously had the love and respect for her daughter to explain Rhys' transition in very simple, straightforward terms.

"He was born knowing," I replied, "Just like you were born knowing that you are a girl." Somewhere in my subconscious I was hoping all this would be explained very matter-of-factly, and she would skip off to her mom and ask if they could get a Happy Meal for lunch. No such luck with this little brainchild. I looked to her mom repeatedly to see if I had gone too far with my responses, but she replied with a reassuring nod that it was okay to explain more.

After a long silence spent thinking about what I had said, the little girl pulled out the big guns and shot this out of her innocent four-year-old mouth: "But *how* will he get a boy body? If he was born with a pee-pee like mine, will he just get a penis? *BUT HOW?* By *magic*, or God, or something?"

She had just upped the ante to the highest level of brilliance any four-year-old could muster. I was feeling less and less adequate at explaining this process to a child. This is actually the first child I have been confronted by about Rhys' being transgender. There was no time to recover gracefully, because she continued, pressing me for more details, "But you're a girl, right? And you have a pee-pee just like mine? And you don't want to be a boy, and you never will turn into a boy, right?"

She was beginning to show signs of exasperation, and it was in this flash of a moment that I realized her fear was based on insecurity about her own ability to retain her female gender identity and female body. Her next question confirmed my hunch. "And I will never just *turn into* a boy either, *right?*" she hopefully asked.

"No", I replied, "Only *you* can decide if you are a boy or a girl, not anyone else." The relief on her beautiful face matched the relief swelling in my heart.

Happily, I escorted mother and daughter down the hall to Rhys' office. As I turned to walk away, I heard the girl ask Rhys, "Is your name T?"

"No," he replied gently, "My name is Rhys."

As she looked from her mother to Rhys, her face again became quizzical, "Then, where did T. go?"

Bless her heart, I thought, and kept walking. It was Rhys' turn to find the answers. I retreated into my office and gently closed the door behind me. It dawned on me how a conversation about gender with a four-year-old was actually pretty amazing. If a preschooler can grasp and accept the idea that gender is partly about self-expression and not solely defined by a genital body part, then perhaps we are moving forward in a big way. One baby step at a time.

Her question did make me wonder and ponder, though: Where *did* T. go?!

CHAPTER 4

Walk Like A Man

~~

April 18, 2006

RHYS IS BEING RECOGNIZED IN THE WORLD AS A MAN more often now. We ventured out to an upscale suburban area for dinner tonight and were ignored by the whole of "upper middle-class" society. This is a restaurant where Rhys was mistakenly addressed as "lady" very recently. Progress—slow but sure.

What I want to know is: Now that Rhys is living in a physical body that more closely reads as male, what was it ever like for him to be in a female body? It is so hard for me to imagine my femme spirit entering into a physically male body. First of all, yuck! Secondly, I'm almost positive I would be perceived as an effeminate gay man. I mean you have to know how to pull it off. (No pun intended!) To reach my hand up to my cheek and feel rough, overgrown stubble would be so foreign to me. I laugh in hysterics at the thought of standing in front of a mirror trying to make my pec muscles "dance." But what would be really mind-blowing is the whole penis thing. From my perspective, men have this incredible sense of internal and external power that is all contained in one small, for the most part flaccid, organ. Yet, there is a constant physical and mental connection to this piece of flesh. Men are forever poking and pulling at their crotches, checking to make sure everything is in the correct location. Is there

71

a correct location, by the way? It would be no less than fascinating for me to experience this foreign obsession. Even for half an hour. Honestly, I wouldn't be able to keep my hands off of it. Imagine me locked tightly in some room, testing out all the different ways this amazing organ can work. I would be tucking and pulling so much, guaranteed I would injure myself in the span of thirty minutes. Though the insight gained would most certainly be worth finding out.

The flipside of this is how Rhys lived his life for 41 years: I can't imagine it actually, Rhys with breasts. How did he ever make it through four years of college (in an all-girls' school!) and four more of professional school with those things attached to his torso?

When asked, Rhys' reply to all of this? "I don't remember how I felt back then." Now that he has transitioned, Rhys says he no longer has the ability or memory to respond to my pressing questions.

April 20, 2006

"OH BOY!"…That was the caption on the T-shirt above the ripe belly of the young pregnant woman who walked into the restaurant where Rhys and I were having lunch.

Where do I begin? First and foremost, we live in a society where it is now commonplace for parents to know the genitals of their child within months of conception. Nurseries are painted and decorated in the apropos colors and styles to fit the "sex" of the much anticipated baby. No surprises left for these births. It would seem these children are given no room to grow into their own gender identity. No place for self-discovery. I must admit, when I was expecting my children, it never occurred to me that they could or would be anything but a boy or a girl. I wonder now, though, what is it is like to be the parent of a transgender child? The other day I was at my friend's house and her five-year-old son was playing with two kids. He introduced his friend.

"This is my friend Maddy, she's a tomboy."

Maddy looked at me and defiantly said, "No I'm not, I'm just a boy." Maddy went on to explain, "I'll never be a girl; girls are stupid."

Here stood before me a wonderful ten-year-old female-bodied

child, who self-identifies in this moment as a boy. What color should "her" room be?

The irony of Rhys' story is that all the pictures of him growing up with his ten sisters, clearly point out his difference. In the Easter photos of the 1960s, all the little girls are donned in pastel tights and crocheted ponchos with matching colors. Shiny Mary Janes and pretty ponytails complete the scene. There, in the midst of the pastel flock is Rhys, so painfully easy to pick out. He is the one with the black hound's-tooth jacket, no tights, and brown Oxford shoes in place of the uniform patent leather Mary Janes. How his mother had the foresight to allow him the freedom of gender expression in 1969 is far beyond my comprehension. That she *did*, however, was an amazing gift. Those pictures are a visual archive of how Rhys has felt about his gender from a very young age.

If we gave every child the same freedom today, how many of us would have a similar photo legacy? The world of pink and blue and the gender binary system it signifies need to fade into our history. I am grateful for my friends who allow their children space for the self-discovery of their gender. No dolls-for-girls, trucks-for-boys mentality. I sense a slow growing awareness of open-minded parents, and hope I live to see the day when the idea that there are only two genders is laughed at.

April 25, 2006

Rhys is becoming part of the "men's club" in ways that I am not sure I want to know. He shares conversations with me (perhaps against his better judgment), that are shocking and sometimes disgusting. For Rhys, it's a catch-22 of sorts. When he is accepted into the male camaraderie, he is so jazzed to tell me about it that he forgets there is a reason that I prefer not to be included in all of the info. I have personally experienced male privilege and chauvinism in the form of discrimination, abuse and invalidation. For some, it may suck to look at an entire gender through my eyes, partly due to the past. I am working on getting beyond it. But I still live in a society where I am often ignored by cis men when Rhys and I are talking to that man. He doesn't ask for my input. It's insidious. And now there is a shift happening between Rhys and me, and it's showing itself in how we understand each other less around our individual gender experiences.

Today Rhys was with another professional man at a business meeting of sorts. Prior to anyone else joining them, the guy shared his most recent "experiences" with women. Rhys assures me he gives no details regarding our intimate life, but the pressure here must be huge. The invisible line of competition is drawn in the sand and the next thing you know everyone is trying to jump over it in order to brag. That's it: a mere statement immediately becomes a competition. So here's Rhys, thrown into the midst of this guy-to-guy conversation, and he isn't struggling too hard to fit in. Single men tell Rhys that they discreetly have their sexual needs met once a month for money. Married guys bragging about how many women they slept with before they became husbands. And in addition he gets that knowing nod from complete strangers that seems to say, "Your woman is hot, good job lad."

I don't know if it's me or if it's being with Rhys, but in my previous relationship I didn't witness this behavior. I must have had on blinders. What I find amazing is that I am noticing there are times I feel threatened by the intimacy Rhys shares with these other men. When he was perceived as a lesbian this behavior was not a part of his existence. Now that he is perceived as a cisgender man by other men, I feel that a piece of our intimacy has shifted. I'm not sure what to do with my new awareness, but if I am honest I'll admit it doesn't feel very good. Things are constantly shifting in our relationship, and I am aware that Rhys has gained something that I will never attain: male privilege. He does seem to be more interested in what the men are doing, and that is new to our dynamic. We used to primarily hang out with other women, mostly lesbians. Now Rhys has found some friends who have transitioned and some cis guys that he prefers spending his time with. The shift is odd, and I'm not sure how to handle it. That privilege allows him into spaces where men share an intimate bond to which I am not privy. I feel left behind.

May 3, 2006

Rhys had an appointment with the doctor this morning, and everything was translicious. His blood work came back in great shape, which was a significant relief to me. I know that it isn't entirely my responsibility; however, injecting the needle into his tender flesh carries great weight for me. If the very serum I inject ended up turning my lover into a "roid-raging" horn ball I would feel devastated.

Not a day goes by where Rhys hasn't called my attention to some aspect of his newly emerging physique. Lately, he exercises with a vigor that can be compared only to his love of peanut M&M's. His ability to build muscle has increased substantially since taking testosterone. His body has changed drastically. His neck is losing the gentle slope where it joined at his back. The girth of his torso from front to back has increased markedly. Because of this, I can no longer wrap my arms around him as easily as before. His brow is heavier, and his face has broadened so much that his eyes and mouth appear smaller in it. And one more detail: Rhys has become one hairy trans man! Hair is sprouting everywhere, and every strand is noticed and counted with immense pride.

I secretly pulled out the pictures of Rhys from the past, before he began to transition. I wanted to remind myself of how he once looked. I need to know that this man in front of me doesn't represent my insanity. The pictures are proof he once lived in a female form. I try not to pine over the past too often. I don't feel like it's healthy for me in this current demand for progression. But that doesn't mean I'm not feeling it. I miss the softness *she* had and wish I could be held by *her* just one more time. I can't tell Rhys this. He would probably think I'm unhappy with his changes, but that's not it. I miss some things about his former female body and the way she presented and moved in the world. This is confusing to me. I don't wish he would be she. I just wish that I would have paid closer attention to his changing body in the initial weeks of his transition. The parts of Rhys' personality that have changed are parts that I now dearly miss: For example, his emotional depth and the ability to see things on a less linear level. How could I have known? He and I are so involved with all the physical aspects of transitioning, that we seem to be carelessly overlooking the emotional ones. Try as I might I can't seem to grab onto the moments where these former characteristics made their magical disappearances.

May 9, 2006

Inevitably a time will come in the too near future when the

memory of Rhys' former body will be vague and unfamiliar, and it will be shocking. I fear this day and close my eyes to the premonition of it. I desperately want to remember all the details he is working diligently to forget. Our journeys may run parallel, but they differ with every step made. I can no longer see "her," and I am afraid of what this means for us. This transformation is becoming increasingly internal, where I had been lead to believe that the physical body would be doing the most changing. I am running to stay astride and not to stumble in the progress.

May 10, 2006

Today, Rhys is going before a county judge to legally change his first name. A few weeks ago when we went in to the courthouse to apply for the change, the guy behind the counter asked,

"So, male-to-female, right?"

We simultaneously turned our heads toward each other in confusion, and then at the same time had the realization that this man thought Rhys was a *male* getting ready to transition to a *female*.

I guess compliments can come in the most unexpected of forms!

Walking into the county court building from the parking ramp, Rhys said that "he feels like he's in some kind of trouble." I guess knowing that a judge is going to quiz him on his motives behind the gender change is getting the best of him. Yet again, the long arm of growing up Catholic has just grabbed Rhys by the scruff of his neck. However, in the end, the whole process lasted only ten minutes. The judge asked Rhys to verify that he had undergone a surgical procedure towards the transition. After that he asked me and the other witness to vouch for Rhys. That was pretty much it. The only visible side effect of the whole experience was Rhys' sweaty palms.

YEEHAH!

Mr./Dr. Rhys!

The court clerk turned out to be a lesbian, and mentioned how happy she was to have "family" come into the court.

"Family?" Rhys asked of me afterwards.

"I hope that family includes me as a trans-identified heterosexual male."

Hmmm…. good point baby, a very good point. Although I can't refrain from a tribute to the judge for including us in her community. Day-by-day I continue to lose this recognition, and it doesn't feel so good. For Rhys this may not matter, but I desire the camaraderie. There are times now when I am with him that I feel transparent, as though my truth is disappearing as his becomes irrefutable. As of now I'm not sure how to navigate this part of our journey. I just know that for me it's still cool to get a shout out from a member of the LGBTQ community.

May 12, 2006

In one month Rhys is taking me out to New Jersey to meet the family. He has been genuinely concerned about my being overwhelmed by them once we get there. Ten sisters and one brother, noted reason for concern. They don't all reside in Jersey, but even if half of them did they could start their own basketball team. I am somewhat hesitant, for many reasons. For one, I don't want to be "the next girl that Rhys brings home," and two, the individual responses to their brother (who not so long ago was actually their sister, or so they believed), could make or break the entire vacation. Just being in public intro-duces more variables for Rhys than any average person would ever care to gamble on. Now multiply that by family dysfunction and divide it by 11 (the number of siblings he has). In order to buffer the impending reunion, Rhys has been writing individually to each family member we may possibly see while in the Garden State. I have sufficient reason to believe that Rhys' new girlfriend (me) is going to be of much less interest to all of them than their new brother.

May 15, 2006

A letter arrived in today's mail at Rhys' house. It was from Dr. Brownstein's office in San Francisco. Dr. Brownstein is the surgeon who gifted Rhys with his fabulous new chest.

Rhys read the letter aloud to me as tears welled in his eyes. The letter (which was requested by Rhys to further the process of achieving the gender and name change on his birth certificate), officially declares him as male gendered. In this moment I can't fathom the validation for Rhys while reading these words written by a surgeon, "Testing has been carried out to determine this patient's true gender. In the case of Rhys this was determined to be male."

The surgeon's letter is the Willy Wonka equivalent of Charlie waving his golden ticket as he enters the Chocolate Factory. There are many persons in positions of power who could try and put an abrupt end to Rhys' transition. Luckily this doctor understands and has compassion for the transgender person. We call these people "gatekeepers." Their positions can range from therapists to doctors, hospitals to the ever so tricky insurance companies. What I have learned recently is that in order for an individual to legally change their gender, a letter must be written by a psychologist that a diagnosis of a GID (Gender Identity Disorder) has been given. In addition, a physician must write and sign a document that some sort of surgical procedure has been performed to indicate the desired change. My question now is this: What if a person identifies as male, is in a female body, and *does not* desire any surgical alterations, or a psychological disorder diagnosis that follows you for the rest of your life? At the present time there would be no open gates for this person to obtain the legal gender identity they seek.

Try and imagine this; your child is born deaf, the doctors know it, you know it, and surely your child is learning every minute that he/she cannot hear. Now try to imagine this; in order for your beautiful baby to receive the care and physical diagnosis needed you must first have them diagnosed with a psychological disorder. Then a physician must verify that a surgery has been performed before this child can receive the diagnosis of deafness. Until this time everything you do as far as care for your baby is financially your responsibility. I know that reading this sounds absurd. Yet this is the very process that is forced upon a transgender individual should they wish to live emotionally and physically congruent. I don't understand the reasoning. As for now, Rhys waits anxiously for the official copy of his legal name change. If he is granted this, he can mail both documents to the Office of Vital Statistics in his state of birth, New Jersey. He will then have to wait to receive (hopefully), a new birth certificate that reads "Rhys," his new first name with the gender listed as "male."

Drum roll, please.

May 19, 2006

The invites read, "Please join us in a celebration honoring Rhys!" And tomorrow is the day! I have arranged for twenty five of Rhys' closest and most supportive friends, to be at our favorite little Greek restaurant to join in celebrating his newness. It's a re-birthday party of sorts. It seems to me if these aren't the moments deserving of celebration, then none are. Rhys has made me promise that there will be no moments during this party where he will be put on the spot. I assured him no, at the same time wondering if that would include me singing a love song to him in front of all the guests.

There are so many ways in which Rhys is physically changing, but perhaps the most disruptive and least desirable is his inability to get a night of uninterrupted sleep. Without fail, he is awake every night for at least an hour and a half. He wakes, sweaty around his neck. His hormone level is doing a dance inside his flesh that requires a new tempo of music. There are so many small (and not so small) changes that no book or medical professional has predicted for us in this. Regardless, between his newly acquired talent for snoring and his sweaty disruptive sleep, I have been all but forced to sleep in another room if I want to sleep at all. I know this is selfish of me, but WAAAHHHH! I want to cuddle up to my lover's strong new body and feel his warmth against me in the night.

Frustration sets the tone of our bedtime ritual. My hope is that since the process of transition is not complete his body will soon settle back into a rhythm that will allow us to share the night. It's pretty wild to be in love with someone who is physically morphing right before my eyes. I mean, over time we all have our changes; a haircut here, some weight loss or weight gain there, but how about this for life altering: first female bodied, now male bodied?

May 21, 2006

Yesterday was the wonderful party that I threw for Rhys to celebrate all of his newness: his birthday, his re-birthday, and ten years of sobriety. It was a beautiful occasion, and I couldn't think of anything more fitting to celebrate than Rhys' courage to become his true self. I love him for that. One of the guests in attendance was the sister of Rhys' friend, a trans guy who recently underwent the first phase of a three-part metoidioplasty, a surgery that creates male genital anatomy. (For those of you reading who do not know what this procedure is, I will refer you to the internet and its vast resources, so as to spare myself the explicit details here.) I asked her how her brother was doing, and her response was less than encouraging. Four weeks post-op, she reports he is still in terrific pain. And this is only the beginning of the suffering. For the first time since Rhys has begun his physical transformation, I feel a river of fear running through my ultra-femme veins. These surgeries and their risks are all too real, and it seems to me that many if not most trans men are all too willing to stare down those risks in order to feel whole. This got me thinking (which can sometimes lead me down a path of no return) about the many risks involved.

I visualize it as a dry goods scale from the early 1900's: on the one side are piled the physical risks involved in altering the female body to male. The list begins with the risks of injecting testosterone on a weekly basis, along with risks from chest reconstruction surgery and the multiple choices for genital surgery. On the other side are the mental and emotional risks due to safety concerns, of being a man in our world, with breasts and a vagina. Not the perfect place to try and strike a balance.

Recently Rhys and I watched an insightful documentary series on the Sundance Channel, "Trans Generation." The program followed four transgender college students: two female-to-male, two male-to-female, on four different campuses across the United States. One of the trans men, a grad student in neuroscience, was attending Smith, a Women's school of great prestige and steeped in generations of female tradition. Along with the many issues he so eloquently struggled with as the *only* male student on the campus of a female college, he was agonizing over the decision to begin hormone therapy. He shared his uncertainty about taking a hormone (testosterone) considering the medical community does not fully understand potential side effects from long term use. I appreciated this guy's uncertainty and pain. As Rhys continues to masculinize every day on the testosterone, he also is dependent on the hormones. What's to fear? I fear the unknown: the effects of the hormone on his cells, on his brain and on his body's vital systems. Every six weeks Rhys goes to a lab for blood draws to check that his body is handling the testosterone. So far everything has checked out just fine. But what are the long-term side effects? Even the doctors we have talked to don't seem to know for sure.

Well guess what? Despite the fact I have not talked to a lot of doctors who specialize in hormone treatment for trans men, I don't like the vagueness around the long term effects of testosterone. As the testosterone adds to the changes in his physical appearance, what dormant problems could be lurking below his flesh? I have so many questions to ask and seemingly nowhere to search for the answers. I'm particularly concerned with the lack information on the possible risk of cancers involved in hormone therapy. Perhaps my own fears around my past experience with a hormonal cancer get in the way of my thinking clearly on this subject.

Rhys' response to my fears is his belief that his cells have longed for testosterone since the day they were formed. He is truly convinced that his former female organs created a greater risk of diseases such as cancer. He feels completely confident in his decision to transition. His mind/body connection should be well served by his positive thought process.

May 22, 2006

The events of transitioning are happening with a speed quicker than I can write. Rhys applied for a new driver's license today. He proudly put a big dark "X" in the box next to "male." The application was processed without event, a new picture was taken, and we were on our way. Sometimes the simplicity of these enormous events leaves me speechless with their irony. As of today, Rhys is legally male. Boom! Just like that. He seemingly just walked through an invisible door to the many privileges of the straight, white male. Twenty-four hours ago he had all the lack of privilege that any woman faces. Yesterday, he could not legally marry unless to a male. But this is a new day, filled with all the attending male privilege.

To be brutally honest, it really pisses me off! I can't help it! I know full well this is my ego rearing its most ugly head, but our worldview of gender and gender roles is so incredibly limited. Rhys is now treated with more respect than I will ever dream of achieving, and what he did to earn it was get rid of boobs and grow a beard. Of course, on a deeper level he has changed much more than just his body, but the world at large doesn't see this. No, they just see a white man, and with that, give him all the Fourth of July-apple-pie privilege that many white men in America expect. As a woman, I have only observed this phenomenon from the outside looking in. To be honest, it doesn't look pretty to me. There is such a clear division of privilege in our binary gender system, and I wonder about a world where a person who was female-bodied yesterday can be catapulted on the respect-o-meter by merely growing facial hair and removing breasts!

Entitlement. So this brings me back to my original digression; I am pissed off that because Rhys is now "legally male" he is given prescribed authority and respect that he previously knew nothing of. My joy for him is overshadowed by this; I feel left behind in my own daily doses of gender discrimination.

May 27, 2006

I found the trans people! I found them! They were all packed into this grungy little art theatre on the west bank of the University of Minnesota. Rhys and I took our two most supportive friends to a screening of a documentary about FTMs called *Enough Man*. In the ninety-degree heat, the tiny, unventilated theatre turned into a literal hothouse and not just because of all the trans boys in attendance. (Wink.) The heat index in the theatre climbed in sync with the erotic content of the film. It was getting hot, and I was getting *hot*! This film depicted the sex lives of trans men in the most graphic visual content I had ever observed. I couldn't help thinking I wished the house lights would come back on so I could take in the largest group of trans men I had ever seen.

This choice of Saturday night fun was originally mine. But as the film subtly grew into trans porn, I was glancing at our friends out of the corner of my eye hoping they weren't offended. Rhys was definitely uncomfortable; I could see it in every shiny drop of his sweat reflected by the soft light of the of movie screen. The energy he was sending me through our clenched hands was screaming, "*Get me outta here!*"

When it got so hot in our fifth row bleacher seat that I thought I would pass out, I knew I needed to make a quick exit. Passing through the threshold of the theatre door into the fresh moving air of the night was like breaking the surface of water after staying under too long. I leaned against the brick wall, disoriented by the heat and what I had just witnessed on screen with 75 total strangers. I wasn't expecting the rush of emotions and thoughts that flooded my body and mind. After a few minutes, Rhys emerged from the tiny door, looking like he had just finished an eight-hour day of bricklaying in the Sahara.

He jokingly commented, "What did you get us into?"

I assured him I had no idea the movie was going to be so sexually scandalous. Surprisingly, our friends waited out the last ten minutes of the flick and came out looking somewhat shell shocked.

Rhys teased, "The suburban housewife brings us to a sexually explicit trans movie…she never ceases to amaze and increase our cultural awareness!"

We all had a good laugh over that and began to walk to the car.

Our friend Lisa then exclaimed in her southern drawl: "Wasn't that a great movie?" and continued, "I loved the interviews with the guys and how honest they were on camera." I was delightfully surprised at how she had received the explicit content of the documentary, but I felt compelled to share my true feelings about what I had just observed. With my brain still swollen from the temperature in the theatre, I did my best to put into words the jumble of thoughts and feelings I had boiling up (literally) within me.

The trans people involved in the film were all in the same general age group of approximately eighteen to twenty-five years old. They represented a cross section of ethnic and socioeconomic diversity. Because of their ages, however, I felt that a large population of trans men were overlooked. I am happy that the majority of people who will view this film will be people in the transgender and LGBTQ community. The person who announced the movie made the comment that this film is groundbreaking in that much is said about being trans, but not much about the sex life of a trans individual. In my experience, there is just now beginning an open discussion around what being transgender really means. And because the trans-gender population is most often targeted as victims of hate crimes in the LGBTQ community, there is a great lack of understanding. I am not sure the most realistic initiation into the life of a trans person is to have a handful of trans identified people fucking on screen. I grew up in the suburbs, and any form of gender expression that includes an open view of sexuality is not well received in the land of ten thousand churches.

There are many transgender men professionals, who contribute to our society in a variety of phenomenal ways. I am beginning to realize an unnerving trend in the trans community where too often transgender people are portrayed in an overtly sexual way. I am concerned about how the community is presented. I am not certain films with exaggerated sexual overtones like the one we saw tonight are the best educational strategy for our cause.

June 4, 2006

Rhys opened a new window into his past today. He shared a memory with me.

As a child he wanted desperately to be near his father anytime his dad was working on the family car, but Rhys was turned away by his dad. After all, Rhys was a "girl" then, and girls in the 1970s had no place in automobile mechanics. He obeyed, even without understanding, and sulked away from his dad. He missed so much of what would have naturally led him into his own manhood. He wanted to be a boxer, to work with wood, to pee standing up; anything using his hands. His father's response was consistent, "No way in hell."

When Rhys remembers and is honest then, every gain in the process brought an unequal and greater amount of losses. Sometimes the memories come in the form of painful recognitions of what never was. An intangible grief sometimes rises to the surface and offers itself as a means to healing. What's beautiful to me is that Rhys opens himself to these possibilities. It seems that the present has a gentle way of healing the past.

June 8, 2006

I ran into an old friend this afternoon. She asked how this whole "situation" is going for me. I assumed correctly that she was speaking of Rhys' transition and my relationship with him. Specifically, she wanted to know, "Were you a heterosexual, then a homosexual, and now a heterosexual again?"

Questions about my sexual preference are so difficult for me to answer. Sometimes I don't answer, but when I do I find myself inventing a new response for each and every one. I feel I have to first consider the source and determine my reply accordingly. Is this person educated? Religious? An ally of human rights? Do they believe in equality? Are they judgmental? Homophobic? If they're homophobic or judgmental, I choose not to go there.

Quickly, I put together a reply that requires no personal labels, and at the same time respects and protects my relationship with Rhys. I responded by telling my friend that I no longer use sexual stereotypes to describe myself. Personally, I don't feel that I was ever "exclusively heterosexual," even though physically I lived in a monogamous relationship with a non-trans male for over twenty years. "Homosexual" would also be a stretch for me. By literal terms, that would put me as a woman who is exclusively attracted to other women. Not a fit either. Now having loved a female-bodied person and then loving that person through the transition to male, I guess that I would self-identify as queer. Other words for queer are found in the thesaurus. They include: bizarre, unusual, peculiar, weird, freakish, unnatural, puzzling, perplexing, eerie, spooky and on and on. Choose a word, any word, but don't expect that because it fits your definition of my sexual identity, it will do the same for me. We are multidimensional beings, linguistically indefinable in our magnitude. The human language isn't adequate to describe the intangible, and my sexuality is just that: INTANGIBLE. But I choose to keep the majority of this vulnerable information to myself and reply to questions of a sexual nature as vaguely as possible.

Through the experience of being repeatedly quizzed about my sexual identity, I now clarify my response: I do not qualify my sexual identity based on who I am partnered with. What is me is me, and being with Rhys doesn't change that fact. I do not believe that the majority of people have been educated or gifted with the knowledge of gender fluidity. Most have not begun to venture to that place within themselves to explore the basis of their sexual attractions and desires. Therefore, many may fail to realize that perhaps their attractions and desires can change over time. Our culture, being steeped in religious belief and tradition, does not allow a great amount of variance from the heterosexual binary. Anyone bold enough to search within themselves who discovers that they don't fit within traditional norms is immediately set apart. I am from suburban/conservative America where this kind of individuality can get you ostracized from your family *and* community. In my own experience I had to choose between my true self or keeping my family of origin. At this point, I refuse to diminish myself as anything other than what comes from within me.

June 9, 2006

Rhys is having second thoughts about our visit to New Jersey tomorrow. Apparently, not everyone in his family is fully accepting of his transition. He has a sister that is about seven years older. She was present and supportive for the ceremony he shared with his last partner. She participated as a reader. She had no qualms about Rhys being a "lesbian." His being transgender, however, appears to reach the limits of her Catholic understanding.

Rhys' letters to each sibling went unanswered by some, supported by others, and, in this one case, responded to with utter disdain. There was no direct reply. Her words and thoughts were so full of disgust that they were no better expressed than through gossip. She discussed Rhys' newness with the other siblings and stated that she did not understand why he would do such a thing. Her two young children, Rhys' niece and nephew, were also brought into the mix.

"I don't want "*them*" to be around *that*!" she spewed.

That?

That!

She has resorted to calling her own beautiful brother "that"?

We were devastated when we caught wind of her words and feelings. News travels fast when it's nasty. Rhys began trying to dissect how his sister could possibly have gone from being supportive of his earlier choices to being disgusted by his most pure truth. I tried to gently remind him that these are her issues, and we are left to wrestle with our own pain around them. I guess statistically speaking one out of eleven with blatant disgust isn't bad odds. But we are talking about family here, people who grew up in the same places of pain, and who rallied together for survival. This specific sister is the very same one who tried without success to school Rhys in the art of walking "like a girl," instructing him to pull his arms in closer to his sides when he walked and roll up his sleeves instead of pushing them up. She eventually gave up in his pubescent years, leaving him to his masculine, tomboy mannerisms. It appears she has also given up on him now, however this time with disdain.

As Rhys and I share our feelings and our fears about seeing the family, we realize that it is most important to remain focused on those in the family who *do* support us. Rhys' siblings are no different from other people who have not been exposed to transgender people. I guess we have to give them as much time for understanding as we would anyone else, perhaps even more

June 11, 2006

I'm wrestling with my own slow growing anxiety about this trip. It festers up in me like an emotional boil every time I hear "family." First and foremost, I have come here to meet some of Rhys' eleven siblings, numerous nieces, nephews and cousins, and they are to meet their brother Rhys for the first time. Yeah, you might say I have some anxiety about that! On a more personal level, I am going to be intimately involved with a family for the first time since I lost all contact with my own family of origin three years ago. YIKES!

Both Rhys and I had the foresight to know that staying in a hotel while visiting was priority number one. Unfortunately, our plan quickly backfired when we checked into our "quaint little beachfront hotel." Beachfront? Yes. Little? Absolutely. Quaint? Not a snowball's chance in hell. A dripping faucet, a bed with a trough down the middle, and a glaring neon light outside the window. Rhys and I proceeded to fuel a heated 1am argument filled with angst. After acting like teenagers in an old-school verbal fight, we finally patched things up and got back to sanity. Rhys was pretty freaked out about the possible outcome of the next day's "family gathering." "Family" and "gathering" feeling like an oxymoron. Too many relatives, far too many variables. We talked late into the night, and got an exaggerated three hours of sleep on the couch-turned-futon.

When we woke from our "long nap" I devised a plan. We checked out of the quaint little night from hell by feigning a family emergency, and Rhys and I drove a half mile down the beach to a five-star resort, where we secured an overpriced but much appreciated ocean-view hotel room.

The family picnic was to begin at 2pm but Rhys wanted to arrive early, hoping it would curb his anxiety. His sister Patty was hosting the broo-ha-ha at her home in Redbank. Patty is Rhys' oldest sibling, and has been a wonderful and nurturing presence throughout his life. We knocked on the door, and Rhys anxiously let himself in with an urgency to get to his sister. They met in the dining room and were in each other's embrace before a word was said. Now that's what I call love. There was no need for Patty to take a moment to examine his new look, she was loving the person she has always loved, Rhys. This was a promising beginning to a litany of introductions. Two more of Rhys' sisters showed up and were just as accepting as the first. All three had abundant praise for Rhys' transformation. There were tears from every eye, mine included. It was a gift for me to be present at such a loving reunion. As they folded him into their nurturing embraces, no words were required for their complete acceptance of him.

We situated ourselves out on the deck, and were chatting with family while we waited for each new member to arrive. Rhys' niece showed up, who is nearly the same age as him. Because he is the second youngest in a span of siblings that spreads over 21 years, his oldest sisters have children who were born around the same time as Rhys. She was hesitant and quiet, and I caught her stealing long glances at him as often as she could.

Finally, Rhys said to her, "So, Colleen, what do you think?"

She waited a minute to respond, and in a probing manner replied, "I have questions."

I know that on some level Rhys was delighted to have such honesty presented to him.

"Bring it on," he said to her.

She asked about his physical changes and the future of his process. He answered each question as honestly as he could, without going so far as to describe his genitalia in detail. Albeit, she did come right out with the million-dollar question, "And what about the penis?"

I stopped as if frozen in time while I waited for Rhys' response, wondering if she would get the full-on tongue lashing that so many have endured for their lack of boundaries. However, the moment passed, and Rhys answered in kindness that his options were many and that he was undecided on the issue.

Rhys' sister, who had no difficulty accepting him when he was living incognito as a lesbian, refused to attend the day's festivities on the basis that "she just doesn't understand why he *had* to physically change."

Rhys' one and only brother, another misunderstanding skeptic, was the next to arrive. He is also Rhys' senior by eight years. Immediately, his nonverbal energy spoke of discomfort and confusion. His wife wouldn't come near the area where Rhys and I were seated. No matter, Rhys' greatest goal at this point was to reconnect with his family as a man.

With his eyes to the ground, Rhys' brother said, "I just don't understand."

I'll give him this: at least he showed up to say that much to Rhys in person. He took a risk. Who knows what it would be like to see your "sister" three years ago and now be reintroduced to that very same person as your brother? Who knows? I am more than sure that there is unspoken grief for some of Rhys' family in feeling they have lost that other person, their "sister." However, even after a lengthy and anatomically honest conversation, his brother couldn't find anything other to say than, "I don't understand."

I felt trapped at times during this family reunion. Each time we were introduced into a situation involving people from Rhys' past, the tension level tipped the scales. There was a twisted sense that after being carefully scrutinized, we were waiting for some seal of approval. Even dogs are more accepting to one of their own. If a new mutt is introduced to the pack, there is an initial tense moment of butt sniffing but then they all run off and have a grand old time. It seems so simple. But it almost never is.

We continued to put ourselves in situations hoping to educate people and gaining support. It seemed a fine line, and one mention of the penis pushed Rhys right over the precarious line to the side of discomfort. Today, we walked away without any reward for our vulnerability with Rhys' brother. What I wish we could have been privy to were the conversations that took place *after* we left. Those honest and raw comments made in hushed tones in our absence would be the best indicators of those who support Rhys and those who most definitely do not.

June 18, 2006

We have returned home from the beautiful Jersey shore, and are left to sift through our feelings away from the distraction of Rhys' family. I am currently sorting through mine, and trying to understand the intensity we shared while on our "vacation." Actually, my therapist tells me this: When travel involves visiting family, it is not accurately described as a vacation, but a trip. I clearly see her reasoning in this. Never in the history of our four-year relationship have we had more heated arguments in the span of seven days. We were spewing all over each other and leaving the other with cleanup duty. We argued about food, family, sleep and sex. We literally argued about anything that came up. I realize that the stress of seeing his family was the biggest piece in all of it. They are wonderful people and get the utmost respect from me for their attempt to understand and embrace Rhys' newness.

Beyond that, I am realizing that we have been thrust forward into a place of being regularly on display as an "out" trans couple. I feel that I am continuously required to navigate the terrain of what and how much to disclose to whom and when. It can be rather exhausting, and honestly there are times when I don't want to live in trans-land. At this point we spend a lot of time discussing, arguing over, educating, learning and living, the topic of being transgender. It stresses our relationship on many levels, to the point where I just want to be alone.

How much of this to tell Rhys, and what to keep to myself will be my newest undertaking. Sometimes it feels like there is no space for what I am feeling right now. The transition feels so BIG. Rhys requires a lot of attention and validation from me, and at times misses the subtle clues I give him that I need the same. There is not an abundance of places I can turn to for support; in fact, there are very few. My closest friends often gape in fascination (or stare blankly), when I embark on one of my trans tales. I don't fault them for this.

The whole situation is quite atypical, and if *I* flounder in the midst of it, how do I expect anyone on the outside to understand?

I intend to enlist the help of my faithful therapist. She has a way of cutting through the crap and opening me up. Blessings on psychology.

June 22, 2006

Oprah has identical twins on her show today and one of them is a transgender man. From the start, the dialogue was peppered with the incorrect use of language to describe a transgender person. The questions being asked of the transgender guests were hard for me to digest: "So you have lived your entire life as a woman, and one day you decided to become a man?" Oprah prodded.

"*Decided?*" I don't believe that gender is much of a decision. Trans people don't finally *decided* to become male or female. Remember, gender is about more than genitals. It is an intangible characteristic in all of us that cannot be physically measured or absolutely explained. Therefore, trans people do not *decide to change* their gender. The only choice would lie in the decision to change their sex or the physical characteristics of their body, or the way that gender is expressed. I can tell you with absolute confidence that Rhys did not wake up one magical day and decide to become a man. As he describes his experience, he was always male and his physical body did not represent his gender identity. The gender he was *assigned* at birth does not correspond with his gender identity.

Unfortunately, it appeared that a few of the guests on the program weren't very prepared for the intensity and personal nature of the questions they were asked. All this unfolding in front of millions of viewers! The trans man who was asked the question by Oprah looked like a deer in the headlights as he fumbled to explain the depth of his feelings. I can imagine the inner turmoil experienced as this trans guest was on display for all of America, and unable in that moment to verbally express the incongruence he had felt over the span of an entire life! As the show progressed the questions came like bullets; I'm sure each one represented what was collectively on the minds of the average viewer. Oprah has an amazing ability to use diversity in her interviewing process. She is obviously skilled at the process of interview. We are talking *Oprah* here. Oprah then said, "I've done a lot of shows, and I have seen and heard just about everything, but this is something I just don't get."

June 27, 2006

Yesterday I was working with a client, a resilient woman about 72 years-old. I was telling her how helpful it was to attend the Gay Pride celebration last weekend. I explained to her how I thought the booth for T-men, a local group for transgender men, and for LGBTQ writers will be great resources for my personal and professional needs. She looked completely bewildered by what I had just said.

"Why was there information about being transgender at a celebration for gay people?" she asked. "After all, Rhys is not gay." She added matter-of-factly.

How refreshing! Here is a woman born in the 1930's, an era of great discrimination and racism, stating so clearly what is often overlooked by the LGBTQ community.

Why then are transgender people included in the LGBTQ community? Transgender isn't a sexual identity; it is a gender identity. There are, without a doubt, gay, lesbian and bisexual people who are also transgender. But there are also transgender people who identify as heterosexual.

I explained to my client that the "T" in LGBTQ stands for transgender.

"Does this make sense to you and Rhys?" she then asked.

"No, it really doesn't," I replied, "But I think that the transgender population is included in this group, because society doesn't have a clear understanding of the difference between gender and sexuality."

"Well," she said, "You better make sure to write that in your book so everyone can read it and learn more about people like Rhys."

I felt the sting of tears in my eyes. The simplicity of how she communicated this seemingly complicated issue made me weep. I wish that for the sake of Rhys, myself, and all other members of the transgender community, there might be this kind of base level understanding.

At the dinner table this evening, over much reminiscing of the past six months, Rhys looks up from his chicken breast and says, "You know...it takes someone really special to be partnered with a transgender person, someone who is all about love. That's who you are, Ali."

His validation does amazing things to ease my pain in this constant process of change. At times, it's difficult for me to accept his appreciation. I don't want him to feel for a second that I compromise myself in order to be with him. I love Rhys, and Rhys is transgender; it is what it is. On the other hand, however, increasingly I feel strained in my ability to persevere through this process. Sometimes it's because Rhys can (and does) act like a testosterone-raging-asshole, but also because there aren't many support resources for partners of transgender individuals. It feels good to be reminded by anyone that what is happening is not typical for most but at times the process is extremely hard. I feel best when the validation I need comes directly from him.

CHAPTER 5
What About Me?

July 13, 2006

A FEW HOURS AGO, I met Amy Ray, half the dynamic duo of the Indigo Girls. *Flashback...*

About fifteen years ago, I was introduced to the music of the Indigo Girls and instantly became an addict of everything Indigo. Their CDs were the only music I listened to. I learned every word to every song and knew the "Amy parts" and the "Emily parts" verbatim.

ADDICTION!

Even my eight- and four-year-olds knew the words to "Galileo"! I attended the Swamp Ophelia concert and was immediately smitten with Amy Ray. Her candor on stage kept me captivated with the memory for months after. Soon, I began to make some deep connections between my innocent fantasies of hanging out with Amy and my uncanny ability to befriend every lesbian in the northern suburbs. Amy was more than just a passing crush for me; I was actually attracted to her.

How could this possibly be?

All this time as a hetero-homemaker I was harboring subconscious desires for guitar playing butch women? My fetish for all things Amy spilled over into my nocturnal consciousness. I began to dream that

Amy, Emily, and I would hang out and chat on a regular basis. It was that kind of dream that was embarrassing to talk about the next morning; yet, I was tragically disappointed to wake and find that my reality did not include backyard BBQs with "The Girls."

Fast forward to today....

Rhys and I are driving down Franklin Avenue headed for his house. I glanced out my window and caught a woman walking up the street in my peripheral view who looked like Amy Ray!

"Rhys, baby, please don't ask me any questions right now, but please circle the block as fast as you can, I think we just passed Amy Ray." The sentence babbled out of my mouth like a breathless teenager.

My trans boy floored it around the block and came back onto Franklin Street just in time to pull up next to her. And it was her! I had been prepared for this moment by ten thousand dreams and thoughts...and all my dreams and thoughts rushed right out of my star- struck brain as I leaned out the truck window: "Hey, are you Amy Ray?" I was so nervous and my voice was shaking so badly that my words sounded gargled.

"Yes, I am," she replied in that melt-your-skin-off-your-bones voice of hers.

And here's the clincher: All my awestruck intelligence could muster was, "I love your music!"

What? Oh my God! I am such a glorious idiot! "I love your music?!"

Dreams, fantasies and temporary moments of obsession and that's all I could come up with? I missed my golden opportunity to actually dialogue with the one celebrity I have ever remotely cared about. What I wanted to say was, "Hey Amy, I started listening to your music about 12 years ago and it brought me to a place of truth within myself. It helped me realize there was so much more to me than the life I was currently living. I wondered could you possibly fulfill a life dream for me, right here and now? Could you sing one line from "Pushing the Needle Too Far," where your voice goes into its lowest, sultry register? Could you do that for me, pretty please?" (Eyelashes batting.)

Sometimes you just have to wonder why things happen the way

they do, when they do? Maybe she was just walking there, and we happened to drive by at that exact moment. Maybe it was a universal gift given to me to acknowledge my newness. Who the hell knows?

As we pulled away, Rhys looked at me laughing and poked, "Get out of the truck, you're such a lesbian."

July 15, 2006

"Tits For Sale"

That's the caption I read while paging through the most recent issue of *Lavender Magazine*. Below the event description of "a fundraiser for chest surgery," I saw a picture of a young trans man with his head hanging down so as to hide his face. He was naked from his chiseled waist up, with his hands covering the two parts of his body he was obviously selling. Tits. It was so painful to look at, it moved me to tears. My gut wrenched with pain. If today I woke up and realized that I had been born with an extra organ on my body, I would go to the medical community for help and my health insurance would most likely cover the entire bill. Can you even imagine if people with brain tumors had to take out billboard advertisements to raise money for their greatly needed surgeries? I truly don't understand how this is any different. In a society where we constantly and cruelly refuse to include anyone of diversity in basic human rights, we put forth the insidious, negative energy that is being returned to all of humanity. So I tore out the colorful advertisement and showed it to Rhys. He was shocked. I insisted we had to attend and meet this bold young transman, and Rhys wholly agreed.

The beer bash fundraiser started at 5pm on a Saturday night. We had a prior formal event to attend, so Rhys was spiffed up in black dress pants and a starched white dress shirt (yummy...), and I was in a vintage 1940s' cocktail dress. Definitely overdressed for the casual gay bar we were about to enter. There were a few cars in the parking lot, and we both felt a bit nervous as we got out of the truck. We don't go to bars very often.

We had discussed earlier how much we would donate to the young man's pressing cause and agreed that a hundred dollars would be helpful. Rhys had the check in his pocket, and we walked together toward the entrance to the ramshackle bar. Inside, there were a handful of people, 5pm being far too early for the serious partying to begin. The heads turned from every direction and someone behind the bar asked if we were looking for someone. I saw the looks. We were being read as a straight couple in a bar for gays. Invisible again. After explaining to the bartender that we were there for the fundraiser, we were directed to an outdoor patio of sorts. Back out in the sunshine we came upon a group of young twentysomething people hanging out at a picnic table talking. They all checked us out; I saw them. But no one made the slightest move to greet us. We asked if we were in the right place for the fundraiser, and a cute guy, twentyish, stood up and announced the party was for him. I hadn't recognized him because his face was turned down in the ad, and the rest of his body that had been visible on the glossy paper was now covered up. He looked puzzled as to why we would possibly have come to an event such as this.

Rhys spoke up, "I wanted to meet you and to let you know that I support you."

The guy still seemed perplexed as Rhys added, "I understand your predicament, because I'm trans too."

It was as though Rhys had spoken to him in a magic code, and every person present released their true selves, the ones they had been hiding since we walked in. They couldn't believe Rhys was a trans man. The young guy kept staring in amazement at Rhys. I quickly realized that many young trans guys were there, and most of them were pre-transition. They had tight binders around their chests that could be seen through their tank tops on this hot summer evening. One guy had created makeshift facial hair by dotting his face with what looked like black eyeliner pencil. To the average eye this would not have been detected but because of my exposure to trans men (and their secrets), I understood immediately the person was trans. They were incredibly shy and openly grateful at the same time. Both Rhys and I sat down and talked with many of the young people there. Not only were there trans guys, but their partners and girlfriends had come to support their friend's quest to fund his chest reconstruction.

Because of our age and professions we aren't often around this young, vibrant population of the transgender community. In fact, I would have to say that this was the first time we have *ever* mingled with the twenty-something crowd. I was amazed. The women I talked with who are partnered with trans guys brought up all the same issues that I was experiencing: witnessing their partners being "Ma'am-ed" in public, having to drive across the city to find a safe bathroom, and constantly dealing with the repercussions of a trans man who doesn't identify with his physical body. The glaring difference between us was class; they had few financial resources to pay for the surgeries and hormones to begin transitioning. In that moment, I was wishing we could have written out the check for one thousand dollars instead of one hundred! When I look into the eyes of these young trans boys, their pain leaps out at my heart.

In many situations I have also be an outsider in my life. Thankfully, this was not one of those times. The camaraderie I felt with these courageous, beautiful young people was like being part of a family. Our family.

July 20, 2006

Today we visited one of the places Rhys used to work before he transitioned. This was a bold step for him since he was just starting to identify outwardly as male. A woman walked by Rhys, turned, and did a double-take when she realized who he was. Preempting her from calling him by his old name, Rhys started their conversation on his own terms.

"I'm Rhys now," he said, as he held out his hand to introduce himself to her. "I've transitioned."

In response, she replied, "So, you decided to hang up your eggs, huh?!"

Rhys was shocked and retorted, "I never had them in the first place!"

"Wow," the woman responded, "That is so *funny*! Well, good luck to you."

"Ha, Ha," funny, or "You-are-really-weird-and-I-don't-understand-you," funny, I wondered, as she turned and walked away

As time passed, I became more pissed off over the careless

comment. It would be easier if I could let these thoughtless retorts roll off my back.

But for the life of me, in those moments, I just fucking can't!

First of all, who says things like that? *Hang up your eggs?* Sometimes when I am subjected to witnessing these types of idiocies, it feels like I'm back in junior high. The kids who wanted to hurt you would find the most personal way possible to make a comment, then add a distorted twist. The woman's comment felt just like that. The blatant disrespect in her words is a further testament to how little the public understands Rhys' pain. It has to be ignorance because I need to believe that human beings who understand another human being's emotional pain would not dream of making such a hurtful comment. I want to hope that, for the most part, people will tread lightly on each other's vulnerabilities, if they understand them

The other piece of this affront is that the woman can't begin to realize the impact she just made on our lives. Like I said, I should learn to blow it off. After all, I'm sure she did just that. She made her smartass comment, walked away and went on with her day without another thought given to what she said. If we could be so lucky! Because try as he may, Rhys can't help but go to that horrifying place where he critically examines himself and second guessing his masculinity based on an indiscreet comment offered by a woman who we will probably never see again. I spent most of the afternoon reassuring him that this is about her, trying to take the emphasis off what she said and placing it on who said it instead.

July 24, 2006

My seventeen-year-old son has been spending an increasing amount of time with Rhys and me. He adores Rhys. He is desperate for a male role model in the emotional void left by his own father and looks to Rhys to fill some of the emptiness. The teenage hormones run at an all-time high when Rhys and Eli are together; Eli has this tremendous urge to constantly wrestle Rhys. It's pretty amusing when I witness my boyfriend throwing my gangly teenage son over his shoulder, or pile-driving him into the couch. Eli has always responded to Rhys' masculinity, even before the transition began. I can feel his energy toward Rhys and it is all male-to-male. It's all fun and games until Eli, in a fit of laughter, mis-genders Rhys while trying to place the blame for a recent attack of farts. If you want to see Rhys go from the confident, masculine doctor, to the unsure, hurting and withdrawn transman, just one word is required: *She*. Or "Her," Those two words are poison in Rhys' world.

I'm torn about how much to involve myself on behalf of my son. As Rhys takes immediate personal offense to anyone mis-gendering him, it can be very difficult to try and be the voice of reason in these situations, particularly this one. I have tried my hardest to explain to Rhys that when people make these mistakes about his gender it is about them, not him. It is apparent to me that our brains become conditioned to memory response, and this applies to gender-identifying pronouns. Therefore, it is not a reflection of Rhys' masculine appearance when people carelessly fuck up, but merely a lack of consciousness in speaking. A brain fart if you will.

In this situation Rhys puts immediate distance between himself and Eli, and again begins the process of self-examination to excavate what part of him still warrants the pronoun, "she."

Then, later, Eli asks me why Rhys is so distant; did he do something to piss him off? So I tell him, and he replies that he isn't perfect but he's sorry.

I try not to mediate the situation between them, which can be hard. I guess if I'm really honest, it comes to this: I desperately want Eli and Rhys to have a strong relationship; it would make us a family. I want us to be a family. And one single word sometimes hang in the balance...

She.

July 31, 2006

This morning we waited in line outside the Social Security office with a large group of downtrodden looking people. We were there so that Rhys could get a new Social Security card printed with his new name and to permanently change the gender on his ID. Two uniformed officers from the Department of Homeland Security and an airport security screener greeted us. More gatekeepers. No wonder some transgender people never legally change their gender.

The proverbial hoops to jump through get seemingly higher with every step. Today, we jump through the hoop of humility once again. We took a number and then a seat and waited amongst the immigrants and the weary who also held a little piece of paper with a number on it.

I have incredible anxiety in these situations and an increasing need to hide it from Rhys. I have legitimate fears that when he gets called up to the counter, the person working there will realize what he is there for and sound off the red sirens. I am afraid that somehow people will realize that he is transgender, and do something to hurt him or us. I much prefer the controlled environment of our home where we don't have to face all the variables of the outside world. I took a breath as they called our number (gladly not his name, as the mispronunciation most used is "Rice"), and we headed up to the man at the window. He asked for Rhys' current social security card and for the legal documents proving the recent name change. He asked no inappropriate personal questions. After completing the required paperwork, we were told that Rhys' new card should arrive in the mail in two to four weeks. That was it! Once we were back out in the parking lot we were both able to exhale. I had a funny feeling we just snuck through another secret door on the way to Rhys' manhood.

August 1, 2006

Rhys has had a mother lode of nightmares about transitioning. They have become more prevalent and graphic lately. Last night's dream: He was at his old high school and they divided the kids into two groups. He was sent to a room where he had to sew and looked around to discover that he was with the girls. He asked where the boys had gone, and was told they were in the gym. Rhys ran frantically through the school looking for the gym and couldn't open any of the doors no matter how hard he tried. Once again, an outsider, even in his own dreams.

As I listen intently, I realize how grateful I am that he shares his crazy nocturnal cinemas with me. Ultimately, the only thing I can do is bear witness to them. I hope and believe that they will subside along with their intensity, as he increasingly lives and moves toward congruence.

August 6, 2006

Rhys and I are in the process of trying to sell our separate homes in the hopes of buying a house together. This morning I had a phone conversation with our beautiful, gushing, realtor. Gushing over whom? Why, none other than my delicious boyfriend, of course.

As a woman with a rich history of self-hatred and an instinctive sense of self-loathing, I am not at all concerned by the overt sexual energy women (including our realtor) bestow upon Rhys every single day. But seriously, I want to get up on a chair and rave like a possessive femme, "Back off all you would-be trans lovers, he's mine!" "Would be" because Rhys is no longer perceived as anything but a straight male. This realtor has no idea that Rhys has a past posing, I tease him, as female. Rhys and I would like to keep his past private. That is exactly why I felt the wind knocked out of me at the following revelation:

"Hey Ali, I pulled Rhys' property tax records, and I hate to tell you this, but they come up in his ex-wife's name as owner of the house."

"Oh, what name is that?" I ask casually.

"T." (Rhys" given birth name)

Holding my breath and trying to sound natural at the same time, I answer, "Yeah…okay…um, yeah! You'll have to talk directly with Rhys about that."

"Okay, well you clue him in on what's happening here, and tell him I'll call him tomorrow."

"Okay, I'll tell him," I reply, as cheerfully as possible.

(Click.)

SHIT!

Rhys had just gotten out of the truck and was waiting outside for me while I finished on the phone. Quickly, I asked him to get back in the truck. I told him what the realtor had said: that T. was his ex-wife. Just as I had *not* expected, Rhys entirely lost himself in contagious, eruptive laughter.

"That's the best thing I've heard yet!" he wailed. He tried to talk through his tears of laughter, "I am my own ex-wife!"

Next was a trip downtown to the property tax office for the City of Minneapolis, In addition to getting a new birth certificate, driver's license and social security card, we have visited numerous other places completing name and gender change paperwork. Just when we think all of the proverbial bases are covered, some sassy real estate agent brings Rhys' "ex-wife" into the game. All day I poked fun at Rhys, teasing him that he knocked off his "ex-wife." And he was right in there making sick jokes about how he overtook her (like the creature erupting from the gut in Alien), and made her disappear. In the end, he decided to leave it at just that. T. was Rhys' e- wife. The woman of his past who is no longer in his life. The woman he couldn't stand, didn't want to live with another day, and who took seemingly forever to leave.

August 20, 2006

Rhys told me that when all the surgeries are complete the testosterone will become more effective and evident in every aspect. Wait a minute; WHAT?! *More* effective? *More* evident?

In my humble opinion, my road-raging boyfriend needs nothing less than more effective testosterone results. Here are some supporting facts:

1. He currently connects to anger quicker than anyone I know.
2. If he is within twenty feet of visual contact of my bra, he hollers…"BOOBIES!"
3. I already have a teenage son.

I don't believe this indicates a man who needs more effects of testosterone! Most times, I don't even know how to respond to his recent retro-plummet into male puberty. I just stand in frozen astonishment. I am dumbfounded by the rapid digression that has taken place in Rhys' previously stoic personality. How is a forty-two-year old woman supposed to behave in the presence of her emotionally eighteen-year-old lover? Difficult not to feel like Mrs. Robinson at this point in the process, and believe me sometimes I do. But this has to be only the beginning phase of transition; I don't want to get too emotionally freaked that I might be permanently partnered with a frat boy. Gently, I remind him of how he used to approach me physically; the Daddy in our butch/femme love affair, a topper, large and in charge. This has insidiously shifted over time however. And yet no matter how compassionate and considerate my delivery, he feels he's been chastised by "Mommy." EEEWWW! What this all leads up to is a whole shit load of communication confusion! It seems that neither he nor I know quite where to go from here. Currently, we're in a place that I would label awkward.

He also said that he can still feel his body going through some kind of cycle. This whole thing is a huge guessing game at times. Even the doctor continues to answer our multitude of questions with, "We just don't know." It's one day at a time at this place in the game, one bold day at a time.

August 21, 2006

Rhys has decided that in the future, if he has anything to say about it, no one except those from his past will be allowed to know his history. This decision will exclude most people from knowing his past, because the majority of those relationships have long since faded. It is his prerogative, but I can't help but wonder what this absolute statement will mean for me. I'm already experiencing the tight rope walk of when to "out" myself as queer and when not to. I do not "out" myself when it puts Rhys in a compromised position of being "outed" himself. I only "out" myself when my need for community overrides his need for absolute secrecy, and I feel in a safe environment. If I err on one side, I feel as if I endanger Rhys and the man he is; yet, if I err on the other side, I feel like I sink back into self-denial.

I would never blatantly "out" him in my own self-expression, but I will also not lie about my own truth that took me thirty-nine years to claim. I sincerely hope the decision gets easier to navigate as the process continues. I miss being identified as part of the queer community. It was a short run for me in the first place. When I finally created the courage to claim my queerness, Rhys came to me with his self-discovery of being transgender. No sooner did I emerge from that proverbial closet than the door was slammed back on my face, pushing me to the recesses of a dark corner. I have no intention of going permanently back into the closet, however. Not even for Rhys. My job is to figure out how to go through this process with integrity. Since no one else in my immediate environment is talking about what it's like to be in my situation, I have a path to forge on my own. I don't want to sacrifice my own identity so Rhys can safely have his. Yet, I'm not willing to lose my relationship with him over this issue. I have to come up with a way to honor Rhys' privacy while simultaneously retaining my own autonomy. If only we could live in a culture that understands that one person's identity does not create another's. If only.

August 24, 2006

I had an intense conversation with Rhys this evening. I asked him if he has ever taken the information that he is transgender (something he has only acknowledged for the last two of his forty-two years), and carried it with him, back through the memories of his lifetime, examining the past with the insight of the present. He said he hadn't thought of that. I would hypothesize that it's similar to my own experience of peeling back the layers of self, of looking at the past through the eyes of my own experience. I talked of how interesting that he is heterosexual, and I, ironically, am not.

Think about that.

Rhys is transgender and identifies as heterosexual. I am a cisgender woman and identify as "something-else-sexual." When people used to stare at us, he was the one who received the looks of disgust. I, on the other hand, ironically read as a straight girl, was merely guilty by association. Irony at its finest. I am the one who can love and make love to a transgender person. It doesn't matter to me what form his flesh takes, I will make love to that form. He, however, is very clear that he is only attracted to women. Since he is a trans MAN, that makes him a heterosexual man.

So, Rhys *I know who you are, but what am I?*

Bisexual? Trans-sensual? Queer? Indescribable? This is where the ugly truth of labeling rears its roaring head. Here is a newly emerging group that has no label yet. What are we going to call the trans lovers? Quick, before they all assemble and create some sort of alternative lifestyle for themselves, shouldn't we label them in order to keep them in their place?

My thoughts surprised even myself. I now realize that all that Rhys has gone through and will go through in his transition is merely to become more congruent in his true gender and sexual identity. However, *I* get further away from any kind of modern day explanation as he transitions; and, yet I love him just the same. I feel the same level of sexual attraction now that I had for him when he was in a female body.

I have a t-shirt that reads, "I'm not like the other girls."

I wore it to the gym recently. A man is his 50s approached me and asked, "How so?" pointing to the caption on my shirt. Interesting that he even approached me, as my iPod ear buds were clearly plugged in and blasting.

"It doesn't require an explanation," I replied, which sent him on his way.

If most people know what this means to me when I wear it, they would probably be offended. I love my transgender man, and even more, my queer ass self. What I have known since my childhood is that I am not at all like the other girls.

August 31, 2006

An acquaintance approached me today, wondering how to support a friend in the recent revelation that her son is transgender. Without much thought I found myself spewing out information and shared everything I knew in the way of resources, and answered all her questions as best I could. Then I realized, I know a lot about this topic and generally present it well. I feel myself becoming an advocate for the transgender community. I was so excited to hear of another young person coming out.

Rhys and I often discuss how much easier the transition would have been had he gone through it in his teens or twenties. There is much more information and medical help available for young people who are gender questioning these days. I can't help but wonder if my path would have crossed with Rhys' if he had transitioned at an early age. If he had been given the opportunity of transitioning early on, he would have faced an entirely different set of issues. It is imperative that young people have a place to get the support, education and counseling they need to make informed decisions about transitioning.

Every time I come out to someone new, I have an opportunity to educate them about transgender/genderqueer/questioning people. My friend was grateful that I shared what I knew. "I want to know as much as I can," she said, "So I can help my friend."

These conversations can have a ripple effect in the understanding and acceptance of gender nonconforming people. If only I could be a more vocal advocate for the trans community without betraying Rhys' wishes for anonymity. I'm really confused right now about what my place is. It's hard to find the line between my autonomy and respect for his wishes.

The closet is such a dark and lonely place.

September 7, 2006

It's Thursday. A typical day for my trans man: blood draws at the lab, refill the prescription, visit the therapist, ask your girlfriend to marry you…

WHAT?!

That's right! This is *the* day. Almost four years to the date that we met, he brought me to the place where he initially told me "you're hot," and this time, asked me to marry him. I felt faint. I was irrational and shocked. As he opened the box in front of me containing a ring rivaling those worn on the red carpet, I snapped the damn box back shut! For real!

POOR RHYS! Yes! I said and *yes*, and *yes*, and *yes*!

Our union will be legal and recognized by the government.

Same relationship, different day.

Same person, surgically altered body.

Surgically altered body, different privileges.

Watch out because we're sneaking in!

September 10, 2006

After an emotionally draining day, Rhys called to remind me that I need to give him his testosterone shot tomorrow. We forgot to do it today. I could hear the disappointment in his voice. He announced that tomorrow, with my help, he intends to administer the injection himself. I asked if that was really what he wanted, to which he announced, "I don't want to be dependent on you to give it to me anymore. Besides, other trans guys give themselves the shot every time."

Trying hard not take Rhys' preference personally (with immediate failure), I asked him why. He explained that he just wants to do it alone from now on. I didn't want to let go and felt a sense of loss while also recognizing my own dependency. I knew by his tone, however, that I should leave it alone.

October 7, 2006

A friend of ours was speaking at a LGBTQ sobriety event. Some of those in attendance were part of a group that Rhys used to be in few years ago. He hadn't seen any of the women from the group since he started transitioning. They didn't recognize him without introduction. In fact, they didn't give either of us the time of day, or even a simple hello as we waited to enter the auditorium. The gay men, however, well that's an entirely different story. If they were bees and you had smeared honey all over Rhys' body...Hmmm? He wouldn't have gotten any more attention from those gay boys that night. Which gets me thinking: If sexuality were as easy as "he is straight or, he is gay," then how in God's perfect world can cisgender gay men be so sexually attracted to a man born in a female body?

As the evening drew on, one by one Rhys approached his past with a handshake and a smile introducing himself to his own history. It was a powerful thing to witness. Many of the women whom he had considered himself to be close with were quite cold and had difficulty being in his presence. They seemed to be more interested in his date.

Rhys rarely comments on his feelings in these situations, but tonight there's a look of loss in his eyes that I cannot miss. The timing doesn't feel right to press him about it, but I wish I knew if he ever misses part of his past social life. I know with confidence that right now if I asked, his response would be a firm "no." If he answers "yes," he might convey a glimmer of yearning for a past that he is desperate to eradicate.

October 10, 2006

We are going to try a tricky strategy with Rhys' health insurance company. There is a possibility that Rhys can purchase a monthly health insurance policy and still claim that he needs his next surgery due to "female problems." There is one big, ugly catch though: he may have to go back to his given female name for a short time to make this happen. To up the ante, the stakes in this game are extremely high: twelve thousand dollars out of pocket—our pocket—for the cost of surgery and one night of recovery in the hospital. I have never considered myself a gambler by any means, but Rhys is prepared to go ahead with the risk and deal with the financial consequences after-wards. I hope the odds are on our side. If not, the repercussions mean waiting to save or possibly fund-raise an extra 12 grand. Wanna talk about social injustice for a moment?

October 14, 2006

"Emotional pain is far worse than physical pain," So sayeth Rhys.

He has a newfound fascination with the male form, and I under-stand more and more how difficult this challenge of body acceptance can be for a transman. Rhys offered that "being with women is easier because women are far more forgiving than men." I didn't like that he said that and called him on it right away. Saying "forgive" implies to me that someone did something wrong, something that would warrant forgiving. Rhys corrected himself and said that women are more *understanding*. Whatever.

October 17, 2006

We are back visiting our favorite place, Provincetown, sharing my transman with the throngs of openly admiring gay men. Rhys and I are again marveling at how ousted we feel by the community that no longer perceives us as being a part of it. I feel a growing, ambiguous loss. I fear that I'm back in the world of the heterosexuals. Not to be misunderstood, I have no judgment on heterosexual people. I am simply not one of them. I desire the validation of others who are queer identified who have had to take risks in that identity. I love the risk takers, because they have heard someone somewhere tell them no and they decided to do it anyway. When I go out for coffee with my straight friends they are very interested in hearing about my relationship with Rhys, and anything else I want to say about the queer community. The only thing missing in these conversations would be shared understanding based on similar experience. My friends are, and have been, incredibly supportive with me throughout my journey with Rhys. But just once, I would like to have a dialogue with another person who is in a similar relationship. I feel that longed-for validation would take some of the "crazy" out of it for me. I keep looking for this but I'm really lonely in my current situation and it's starting to show in my relationship with Rhys. Currently, he doesn't seem to have the patience to understand my feelings. After all, everything in his world is all whiskers and muscle progress. I am lonely.

November 2, 2006

Another visit to the trans doctor, only this time we were pleasantly rewarded with not having to report to the OB/GYN department. What a thrill. As promised, the office has set aside a new area that becomes the transgender clinic one day a week. Rhys and I played a game of "find the trans people" on the unsuspecting people in the waiting room. The trans group was mixed in with patients from internal medicine and ophthalmology. It would be hard for any uninformed individual to participate in our game. After all a trans person might need any of these medical services. But not a difficult task for Rhys and me; our trans radar is keen and sharp at all times. I wonder why it becomes an unspoken awareness when another transgender person passes us in public? Similar to the gay community, trans people seem to have a secret camaraderie that even they are not always aware of. Regardless, we were already waiting twenty minutes past our appointment time. Patience is not one of Rhys' strongest traits. The nurse finally called us back, and gratefully she was the same nurse we had been working with for the past year. We love her. She never mispronounces Rhys' name or mis-genders him. We feel her support at all times, and she carefully chooses her battles with Rhys when it comes to required medical procedures.

Small blessings.

Our visits with the doctor are becoming shorter and less frequent as time goes on. At this stage in Rhys' transition the visits seem a mere formality. Physically, Rhys is sailing through the process. The testosterone produces less drastic changes as his body adjusts, and he is feeling great. Over all, it's been pretty incredible watching the way he progresses through this. As a matter of fact, now that I take the time to reflect, it's been nothing short of miraculous the way his body has adapted to this hormonal evolution. A short recap of events:

February 2005: Rhys announces he is transgender and wants to transition.

November 2005: Rhys is injected with his first weekly dose of testosterone.

February 2006: Rhys has his chest reconstructed.

June 2006: Rhys is living in the world as a man.

It hasn't been easy, but it's good to take a moment to look at how far he's come in the process.

CHAPTER 6
She's Not There

November 14, 2006

THIS PAST WEEKEND Rhys dug out a home video from a drawer long forgotten. I'm talking old school VHS tape. It was taken during a surprise birthday party for him—his fortieth birthday. This would have been about two and a half years ago, which might as well have been a century ago relative to Rhys' transformation. He casually popped the tape into the VCR machine—I admit; we still have one! —without either of us giving it another thought.

Break out the popcorn, let's have a rendezvous with the past!

I truly thought nothing of it.

BOOYA! Watching him (her!) on the screen, my emotions ran the proverbial gamut. At once, I was attracted and also petrified. The person on the video before me was my lover, but I had lost some of my memory of his former self. I had begun to live as though Rhys was always 30lbs heavier than me, with a beard and a sexy, deep voice. Despite that, this archive betrays me; the person I was attracted to originally used to inhabit a female body. At the time, I felt his masculinity as much as I do now. Certainly that energy transformed in me and the way I perceived him. But now, watching Rhys on this video, he (she!) seemed comparatively feminine. His (her) frame was so much smaller. And the voice? Oh My God his (her) voice was definitely identifiable as female by other people. How could I have missed this back then? SO BIZARRE! Rhys' face was noticeably narrower, so much so that his eyes appeared bigger in it. On testosterone his brow has come down, and his hair has receded a bit at the temples.

As he (she) spoke on the tape, my heart was tormented by the thought of the man trapped in that female body. The man I now interact with daily in the flesh. I imagined the magnitude of his pain and the immensity of his struggle to become physically what he has always felt as his gender identity! As we watched, I turned and hid my face in his firm, new chest, and silently wept. Being able to see Rhys in his former physical state was like time traveling backwards through his transition. Part of my emotional outburst when I saw the video was profound grief. I haven't talked with Rhys about this. I don't want to offend him. He has worked hard and endured a lot to become the man he is. However, I was reminded of the body I once loved. The softness of his face is now covered by a beard. His nipples (that used to get an instant, charged response) are now scarred and have nerve damage from the surgery. Prior to taking testosterone, Rhys also had sexual patience that played an important part in our passion. With testosterone, however, patience has become a conscious thought process and is easily replaced by a certain the urgency. I don't recall Rhys ever being feminine, but there was once a definite physical softness that has since receded in this transformation. I found myself missing him in his pre-transitioned body and felt ashamed, as though I was taking something away. There's a grief for me in this transition that those who have partnered with a trans partner following transition won't understand if they weren't along for the entire ride. There was a passionate attraction I couldn't ignore when first I met Rhys. His physical softness was appealing to me at the time, and I have since forgotten parts of this. Don't misunderstand me; the fact remains I am actually more attracted to him now that he feels whole within himself. His transition has brought about many changes that can't be seen with the eye…a connection has been made inside Rhys that was previously missing in his life and there is a beauty and purity in that.

November 20, 2006

There is a trans male friend in our lives who is blazing the path for Rhys in this surgical odyssey. Today, he had the final surgery of his transition. He and his girlfriend went to Arizona for the week to undergo this final step in his transition. I spoke with her on the phone after the surgery. She explained our friend was experiencing a lot of pain and that so far the medications weren't stopping it.

Yikes! Rhys is planning to have the same surgery with this doctor in the near future. I don't like the foreshadowing we're getting from our friend's experience. A feeling of heaviness in my gut arises whenever I'm faced with the reality of Rhys' future surgical procedures. I'm scared to death of the amount of pain he may have to endure following these surgeries. And perhaps also afraid of my ability to bring him comfort in these moments. I don't know how I will cope. It's rather ironic, these feelings, because my career history includes a six-year stint caring for terminally ill patients in a local hospice program. I felt confident in my role as caregiver and comforter and yet question my ability to provide the same for my own lover. Perhaps there is truth in the idea that the closer you are to someone, the more it hurts.

November 28, 2006

Am I strong enough to be his woman? Last week, Rhys developed a granuloma (a mass or nodule of inflamed tissue that is usually associated with an infective process) on his butt cheek, at the exact sight of his last injection. Basically it looks like somebody slipped a golf ball under the skin of his ass. It got big and hot and ornery looking. *Not* attractive. After talking with the doctor's office we learned it might be that Rhys has an allergy to the oil that the testosterone is carried in. We went to get a new prescription for the testosterone based in sesame seed oil, versus the cotton seed oil which we had been using. It appears he definitely has an allergy to the cotton seed oil. Not only did he have ass swelling, but the back of his throat mysteriously burns after every injection.

Last night, two days late for his weekly injection, I loaded up a syringe and administered a dose of the new batch. It hurt him. The newness and excitement of the weekly injection has long since worn off. I have been noticing that if Rhys doesn't get the testosterone on a regular basis, it affects his mood in a not-so-pleasant way. Yesterday he was beyond grouchy and the day ended just as it began: with his quick criticism of me and my sulking away to lick my emotional wounds. Something has to change.

I don't believe that we have been adequately prepared by the doctor for all the emotional changes that I fear could take place in connection with testosterone injections. I hear mention of it on The L Word (an HBO series following the lives of sexy California lesbians), and in other documentaries about transitioning, but not from the doctor's mouth. I wish she (the doc) would provide more detailed information to help separate fact from fiction.

It's a damn good thing that I have been blessed with a skilled therapist, because it's a needed reality check for me. It helps me to be accountable for how his changes affect me. Prior to my experience with ovarian cancer in 1990, I was one of the lucky ones in regard to hormonal influxes. PMS was never a part of my hormonal experience. However, I have many friends who come close to a breakup on a monthly basis due to their hormonal hell. I wonder about testosterone. Rhys seems to be all over the map right now, and I truly have no clue how much can be attributed to Rhys' natural temperament of situational stressors and how much is due to testosterone's influence.

December 17, 2006

The dynamic of our relationship is shifting. Rhys gives me a look of total confusion more often now than ever before. It's difficult for me not to take offense by it. I know it's best if I don't. After all, he confuses the hell out of me and doesn't seem to bat an eye at my knitted brow. He now thinks I speak too fast and use too many words to get my point across. I, on the other hand, am offended by his occasional guttural grunting in response to a question. My tears only seem to command the desire in him to "fix" my pain. In the recent past he was content to sit with me in my emotion. We seem like ships in the fog trying to at least wave at one another while we gratefully align our separate courses. I don't know how this is happening but my awareness of it comes in stages. There are times when our relationship appears functional. Then one day I wake up and ask myself, "Who the hell is this guy?"

115

I feel uncomfortable because I'm not sure how to bend in these winds of change without snapping in half. An intense aloneness swells inside me sometimes. I still can't find any support as the significant other of a trans guy. When I do, the connection isn't much of a match since all that we have in common is that one thing. So many of the women I meet are 20 years younger than me and still trying to figure out what their partner's transition says about who *they* are. A necessary journey, and yet not where I'm at in this stage of my life. I want to hear someone—*anyone*—speak to the rawness of emotion when a partner is transitioning from female to male. I want to hear about *all* of it: the humor, the pain, the frustration in the daily living of being with a trans guy.

December 22, 2006

"Out" for dinner. We dined at our favorite urban café with another couple, also trans identified. To my left, a table of six: Six gay men with as many half-empty bottles of booze. As we were munching on our food minding our own conversation, I sensed a change in my peripheral view. The guy closest to me at the next table was pointedly leaning his body in our direction. Not exactly eavesdropping, yet definitely intruding with his body language. I made some smartass comment which only seemed to intrigue him all the more.

"We're trying to figure out what's going on over here," he said, casually waving a finger in our direction.

"Going on?" one of us replied.

"Yeah," he said, "We are wondering what the makeup of your 'little' group is."

The four of us looked at each other with a knowing pact of silence around the transgender issue. Just because these guys were gay didn't mean that Rhys and his buddy needed to out themselves.

"You tell *me* what's going on," I sarcastically replied.

At this point I could not only see, but feel Rhys' discomfort with the direction of the conversation. Yet I couldn't resist, "Go ahead, tell us what you think," I foolishly encouraged.

I wasn't sure at all what these guys were thinking other than their obvious attraction to both our friend and to Rhys.

"Well," he began, "Either you are brothers and sisters, or just a bunch of friends hanging out."

"Wrong." My friend spoke up before any of the rest of us could.

"Then," the man to my left continued with confidence, "Fag, Fag; Hag, Hag," pointing to each of us as he went around the table.

The audacity of this guy! I was shocked into silence at the thought that a gay man perceived me as a faghag. Rhys couldn't bear the imposed code of silence any longer and just when I thought he would "out" himself he grabbed my left hand, held up my engagement ring and snapped,

"Hey, this is my *fiancé*! We're getting married next fall *and* we've been together for more than four years!!!"

I must add here that as this conversation progressed, the table of six was quickly turning into a table of drunks! Four of the five other men had their interest piqued and were now involved in this game of *"who are you?"* Having heard enough, the boisterous gay man leaned over to me with a look of disgusting pity, "Sorry honey, but you don't know what you're getting yourself into, marrying a closeted gay man. He may not know it now, but he will. Believe me, he will." The four of us, having just paid our bill, got up and left. Once outside we began laughing and complaining, simultaneously.

January 15, 2007

One year into this transition and there is still no respite from Rhys', at times, uncomfortable journey.

Not once, not even twice, but three times today he was mis-gendered.

"Thank you Ma'am," one of his patients so carelessly spoke on her way out of his office. One person in particular has been having a difficult time respecting Rhys' new or not so new (we are now 14 months into the "new") request for male pronouns. Oh well, it doesn't happen that much anymore, so "people will be people" and "forgive and forget," right? Please allow me to answer myself: WRONG! The further away we get from the time when Rhys was living in a female body, the more insulting these lapses in respect become. Rhys called me with panic in his voice and no reasonable explanation for why this could possibly be happening. *Now?* After the surgery, the testosterone shots, the agonizing period of not quite passing as male, and yet most often being called 'sir'? This is the raw underbelly of emotion that is left for Rhys and me to sort out. Is it reasonable to repeatedly request to be called "he"? It *is* an issue of respect. *Every* person makes a choice before each word is released from their minds and out through their mouths. But Rhys recoils and wonders whether he is making too big a deal out of the situation. Respect *should* be the baseline common ground for human interaction.

Here is an analogous faux pas: A woman is widowed. Months, then years pass since the tragic death of her husband. An acquaintance who hasn't seen in her in a while yet attended the funeral, recognizes her at the coffee shop. As they approach, the acquaintance blurts out, "Hey, Mrs. Cooper how is your husband these days?" Now you might be thinking: How absurd and thoughtless that would be? Yet is this so different than mis-gendering a person who has been transitioned for over a year?

These female pronouns are constant and painful reminders for Rhys of the life he lived for 39 years in a state of chronic and uncomfortable gender dysphoria. The two of us talk frequently about where we can relocate in order to start with a clean slate of gender identification.

March 9, 2007

There has been a subtle shift taking place in our relationship. Issues that were constantly coming up in our everydayness are now left unsaid to each other. Rhys has suffered from situational depression during the bleak Januarys of Minnesota winters past, but my guess would be that this one goes much deeper than that. He is tired most of the time, and requires a nap every day just to get him through. On average he is awake every night for at least two hours. Often times he will lay with me and the heat radiates from his body like a sweltering July night. It's a tedious cycle of not sleeping from 1am to 3am, and then napping from one to three in the afternoon. I have never been a napper, and therefore much of the time we could otherwise spend together on weekends is interrupted by his nap time.

Our once insatiable libido for one another has all but been

replaced with a peck on the lips before leaving for work. I gently told Rhys how lonely I am for him. I tried to make the issues about me, but ultimately he is the one going through these tremendous changes. He has shared some of his feelings with me yet it's my intuition that tells me there is more to it. Even though in the past the transgender thing was a positive part of our relationship, it now (after transitioning) seems like a barrier. In the beginning of this process, he was so excited to name what he was feeling as trans. But now it seems like he doesn't want to use the word trans. He says, "I'm just Rhys." This part of his life used to be a part of our intimacy and attraction, and now it seems to be floating around above us, untethered. I'm at a loss. A loss to fully understand, a loss to even want to. I don't know how, or if, I should approach him. What was once the most natural attraction I have ever felt has become increasingly painful since putting a name or label on it.

Perhaps the baseline of all these symptoms is this: Rhys needs desperately to have the next surgery. His body is fighting a battle against itself and I am inadvertently becoming a casualty of that war.

Most insurance companies don't recognize transgender procedures as "necessary" and therefore will not pay. How anyone could find this fair is beyond me. I would venture to guess that this is an element of why the transgender suicide rate is so high. The medical system appears to work against them every step of the way. Not only will Rhys and I be responsible for the cost of the surgery and the hospital stay, but also the time off for recovery. Rhys and I are both self-employed and do not receive paid time off for sick time or vacation. The average six weeks' recovery time for this surgery isn't occupationally realistic for Rhys. In the midst of all these changes I am desperately trying not to lose myself. I sometimes perceive his lack of interest in me and blame myself for not being desirable enough. Such bullshit. Sometimes there is nothing I can do and honestly, nothing to say.

Recently, I met a woman at my office who has experience in therapy for trans-identified people. I mentioned my book project and she asked if I could meet for coffee sometime. I was so excited to talk with someone who might be even slightly familiar with the issues I am facing in my relationship with Rhys. She told me that she also has been doing research around the grief process and she mentioned a term I had never heard before: intangible grief. To that I would add *indescribable and indefinable.*

March 31, 2007

Today, I went to some workshops on trans issues. I felt privileged to be in workshops with trans men who were being vulnerable with their thoughts, feelings and bodies. At times, I felt as though I was eavesdropping on conversations never intended for cisgender women. So what did I do? I leaned in closer to make sure I heard every word!

I was touched deeply by each person's story; they answered questions I had from my own experience of Rhys' transition. Now that Rhys has transitioned to "stealth" acceptance, I find myself wondering where the "feminine" characteristics of his personality went that he had before he started testosterone? Are they still part of him, repressed somewhere in his hypothalamus? Or has the hormone overtaken these qualities? Were these feminine traits not a true reflection of who Rhys is, deep down? Listening to these FTMs' personal testimonies has made me realize how much I've repressed my own confused feelings and ambivalence toward Rhys' transition.

As we have journeyed together (and individually) through this transformation, I have forged forward with each and every experience. Sadly, however, I haven't always taken enough time to measure the gains and losses for myself and our relationship. When I finally find the time to confront them, the issues feel overwhelming. A disservice to myself I must admit. I've withheld my own grief in the face of Rhys' masculine gains in an effort to protect him from my own feelings of ambivalence. I want to be supportive and yet desperately need to find validation for my own feelings of loss. It sounds odd, even as I describe it.

I thought every step forward—every needle prick, every surgery— in this process was all for *our* personal gain. And while it is on some level, it still doesn't mitigate the intangible grief that I feel and have pushed down for so long. Only twice have I openly wept in front of Rhys for the loss of the female-bodied person I first fell in love with. Once was the pre-transition video we watched together. Up until now, I haven't had any support to help me through these hard moments. But the workshop was a good place for me to start putting together a network of support.

April 1, 2007

After witnessing the stories of many different trans men, I ache and empathize with the pain that intertwines each and every trans man's journey. It also makes Rhys' struggle within even more tangible to me than it was prior to coming to the workshops. Here we have been given the physical space to feel validated and safe. I don't think either one of us realized until this point how much we needed this type of validation. I came to recognize that much of my own grief and loss has gone unacknowledged for much of this journey. I really do miss some of the characteristics that Rhys had before his transition and in protection of him I have hesitated (a better word would even be denied) the expression of my own experience. There is a lot for me to process here and I intend to give myself the time and attention needed to do just that: PROCESS.

April 3, 2007

Lying in bed, Rhys starts talking about some things he's had on his mind. Since starting testosterone, he shares less about what's going on inside. I'm hyperaware of interrupting him with questions. He surmises that the increases in his testosterone levels make it more difficult for him to find the words that used to come so easily to him, although neither of us is aware of any scientific studies backing his introspective musings. Allowing for as much vulnerability as possible, Rhys explained that the music he heard at the conference made him think about whether he has experienced loss or grief in this transition. When he began testosterone, every physical change was a reason for celebration. Each facial hair was counted and carefully groomed. Muscles were flexed and measured on a regular basis.

At that stage in his transition, Rhys never once said, "Wow, I really miss being in a female body." Now that he's securely on the other side, however, Rhys has offered he would spend some time thinking about his former self. How I struggle with losing her, yet gaining him, and where can I go with these feelings? We both have to decide for ourselves what we have sacrificed, but to look over and see him next to me makes me feel less alone.

CHAPTER 7

Communication Breakdown

~ɔ

April 17, 2007

SINCE THE MILWAUKEE CONFERENCE, my discussions with Rhys have broadened into uncharted territory. Twice, Rhys has acknowledged in the company of others he believes I am the one who has suffered the most loss and experienced the greatest changes in our relationship. This public validation of sorts has opened a place in me that I have not yet traveled to alone. I have realized and said to Rhys that he was never a woman. I believe now that there is no mistake he was always a male, albeit a male on estrogen. This is the man I initially fell in love with. Through this testosterone driven transition he has now become a male on testosterone. Now he's just another guy to me. Some of the characteristics I was so undeniably drawn to in the beginning of our relationship seem to have all but vanished.

How could this have happened so insidiously? Could it be that I'm just now, a year and a half later, realizing my feelings for the first time? Ever since Rhys said he was going to transition, I've focused on being the most supportive, nurturing lover I could possibly be. Doctor visits, testosterone shots, traveling across the country for surgery, all these busy-making activities have kept me focused on one thing: Rhys. And now we have plateaued onto a middle ground, a flat land on the journey of transition. Rhys is in between surgeries, the testosterone is producing physical results, and he lives stealth in every situation. With nothing required to focus outwardly on at the moment, there's no better time for my repressed emotions about Rhys' changes to come up from the depths.

In the last conversation I had with Rhys, he told me that he doesn't remember anymore who he was prior to the testosterone. Again, we watched the video of his fortieth birthday party. He was shocked at how he used to look, sound and act. My lover has a dim recollection of his former self. Suddenly I am aware that I have been (somewhat subconsciously), patiently waiting for these female character traits to return. And in that same moment came the brutal slap in the face of awareness: These parts of Rhys are gone. FOREVER!

May 4, 2007

Today, I asked Rhys if he gets particularly grumpy after his testosterone shot. I am aware that his mood changes may (or may not) always be tied to the testosterone. It's difficult to know where I'm allowed to roam with my questions and when I should edit my thoughts before I speak. I'd just like to know whether he is in a testosterone-risen state afterwards. I don't mean to imply that every single "mood" is turbo charged by his injection. I simply want to know what brings on the sudden darkness in him. Truthfully, he doesn't always know himself or what to say after I ask him these types of questions.

May 14, 2007

There is a scene in the 1980s movie "On Golden Pond" where Henry Fonda is trying to maneuver his boat through a bad area called Purgatory Cove with the help of a twelve-year-old boy at the helm. Inevitably, they end up crashing into a submerged boulder full throttle and are thrown from the boat. Today, I attempted to tell Rhys how I'm feeling about his transition lately. With vulnerability I approached him and asked if we could talk. He said sure, but there was a definite hesitancy in his voice.

He must sense my inner turmoil lately. I know I've been bringing up the topic more than he would prefer. As I began to express my thoughts and feelings, he immediately became defensive and unable to hear or validate my experience. Each time he responds like this, I regret to admit, I swallow my words. They stick like peanut butter. I am aware of how unhealthy this is. I have to find a place where my feelings can be heard, a group or something that will fulfill this aching need in me to express my frustration, confusion and pain. There is a group supposedly being formed for partners of transgender men. Unfortunately for me the facilitator is my friend and feels the boundaries would be too blurry if I participate. She is a licensed therapist and acutely aware of professional boundaries in her practice. I don't blame her but WHAT THE HELL? Even in a city as diverse as mine finding support in this situation has proven very difficult. I am actually considering initiating a league of my own. I'm not confident, despite my own personal experience, I could support everything expressed at such a gathering. Regardless, I need someone to talk to. The isolation I'm feeling is born of a culture where any group outside the mainstream experiences marginalization. Yet, I know there are others who are going through similar changes in their relationships. I just have to find them.

Rhys is spending a lot more time with his "guy friends," an opportunity he has waited a lifetime for. He is so happy. Men fulfill an emotional need in him that was previously only spoken about when he vented his frustration to me. Even trying to write my thoughts here, I feel grossly inadequate.

The past 18 months have brought a whirlwind of physical changes in Rhys: body, name, wardrobe…the entire outward appearance. It has come so fast and with so many accompanying required tasks we have often been hyper-focused on "one step at a time." But at the same time (one small step at a time) Rhys has been changing internally. It's been such a subtle process of change that neither he nor I have acknowledged it.

Until now.

As surreptitious as these changes have been, so has my own process of coming to terms with the reality some things have permanently changed. My gradual awareness and experience of grief has flooded in the back of my throat. Tears are choking me in my weakened attempts to spare Rhys from knowing my own pain in his transition. How can I ever tell him that I actually *liked* some (a lot!) of the things about the way he used to be? He doesn't think he ever acted any differently than he does now. He doesn't remember. But me, I remember. I remember at a cellular level. Small nuances that once drew me in have changed and in some cases have disappeared. And I am lonely for those things. I have been hyper-focused on his transition and have been able to move forward without being aware that some of the changes I thought temporary, are actually a permanent part of his transition. It's neither good nor bad. Rather, it's that I need time to work through my own process, too.

My honesty about my feelings only seems to bring further frustration for Rhys. I believe my unreleased grief is just one of those things. I'm feeling angry also. Every time we begin to talk my tears come too damn easy. My grief is fresh, and it scares the shit out of him. I can see it in his beautiful eyes. I know I need to go somewhere else and grieve. I am also aware that a good therapist is worth a thousand tears.

May 27, 2007

Rhys has now been transitioning for eighteen months. He is seen as male everywhere now. He desperately wants to complete the remaining surgeries so he can put the transition behind us. Yet, he has regretfully decided to wait until the winter to have the next surgery. He's still trying to get health insurance, and even if he does, there's no guarantee they'll cover his transgender health care. The surgery will cost twelve thousand dollars out-of-pocket and recovery time will be a minimum of three weeks.

At times, I feel as though I'm living with someone I don't know anymore. Rhys is content with what I think of as so much less in our relationship. Yesterday I came up from behind him and wrapped my arms around his body. He pushed away my hands and made an increasingly common statement, "I'm a little irritable right now."

It seems to me that any approach for physical connection is met with "irritability" as of late. I haven't been one to let a sleeping dog lie, so I gently tried to confront the subject later in the day.

"Do I irritate you?" I asked kindly.

All he could give back was, "I wouldn't take it personally."

I'm not quite sure how else *to* take it, Rhys.

There was a time not so long ago that his desire for my touch and to touch me was insatiable.

Moving in together while Rhys has been transitioning has blurred the lines of recognition between which problems stem from Rhys' transition and which ones are the result of a couple living together for the first time. Before I moved in with him, I had lived alone for four years and loved every minute of it. We have both compromised a lot in our new living situation. In a parallel line, Rhys' transition has progressed as his body continues to change from effects of testosterone.

Now, six months later, we've passed the adjustment time for shackin' up, and yet some key patterns in our dynamic seem to be permanent. Rhys is easily frustrated with me and much more critical. He meets my emotional vulnerability with his tool kit of "let me fix it," when all I really want is to be heard. Before his transition we were reading everything we could find about testosterone and the whole transition. Everything I read had prepared me for an increase in his libido, and now here I am facing the total opposite. The communication pattern seems to be that I allow some time to pass between spats until I decide it's worth the risk to be vulnerable again. Then my feelings are met with his defensiveness and emotional blocking. Getting compassion and understanding from him is rare. Right now, it takes Rhys a lot of time to tap into feelings of empathy.

Meanwhile, body building has taken a front seat in Rhys' life lately. It has become the main topic of our conversations (with his shiny new truck being a very close second!). His time with my son has increased even further and become a source of great satisfaction for him. Everyone benefits here, and I am enjoying the support from Rhys immensely. After all, try as I might I cannot be a father. Times in the past that Rhys and me would have spent alone have become a threesome—Rhys, my son and me. The dynamic of this trio puts a different spin on everything. Rhys enjoys the make camaraderie with my son as, of course, he does not have any children of his own. The two of them are a perfect match and genuinely enjoy each other's company.

For Rhys' birthday my son gave him a cheap titty-girl birthday card, a hunting knife and a keychain that swears when you push a red button. He also got a wrist rocket from my daughter. No wonder my gift of an antique framed map was met with all the enthusiasm he would have for a root canal.

May 28, 2007

We talked last night and the next morning. Rhys says he gave some thought to what I've been saying and that he couldn't imagine how hard this must be for me. He said this is the point where some couples who transition together break up. I need his validation of my feelings. I need confirmation that I can say his changes have and continue to affect me on a profound emotional level. Validation is the most amazing thing. It changes your reality past, present and future. It's like being handed a life preserver after treading water in the ocean for ten hours; it buoys me.

We met up for coffee this afternoon with an old friend of Rhys'. She has a new girlfriend and this was the first time we met meeting her. Rhys was surprisingly vulnerable with these two women. He shared how he and I have been struggling with some of the deeper issues within his process of transitioning. They were a rapt audience, and he must have really felt safe because he went on to say aloud how he believes his transition has been harder on me than it has been on him. I'm hard-pressed to remember whether it was his tears or mine that followed, which made me fall headstrong in love with him all over again. This is what I'm talking about here, just when I think his bicep circumference is his deepest thought, he pulls a fast one on me. *Validation.*

S.O.S.... I think I see a ship on the horizon.

May 31, 2007

This morning I am off to see Rhys' therapist of the past four years. This could get even weirder. Rhys recently decided that it might be time for him to move on to different areas of support, including a men's group. It was actually his idea that I might benefit from her "inside connection" to his transition. I have great hope that this may be a place where the unspoken can be screamed.

What I thought was going to be an emotional solo flight, turns out to be tandem. At my first visit with her by myself (without Rhys) the therapist felt strongly that my grief over Rhys' changes would best serve our intimacy if shared. She validated that I have a right to my grief and it needs to be heard.

Unfortunately, my need to remember and grieve the female physical traits that no longer exist in Rhys is in direct conflict with Rys' desire to move forward and complete the rest of his surgeries. The therapist believes that it's never healthy to splinter off a part of ourselves. However, she will only work with me on certain issues if Rhys is involved in a couple's therapy setting. YIKES! Sometimes I feel I've bitten off far more than I can chew. Yet, the journey always has an uncanny knack for bringing us to the next destination.

After the session was over Rhys called with great anticipation asking "how much this therapist would help me get through my stuff." I told him as honestly and accurately as I could recall what she had said. I could feel his energy change, even over the phone connection. "I don't know if I want to do this," he said. I was shell shocked, especially since I had just said to the therapist that Rhys would fully sign on to this process. He told me he would have to talk to her and think about it some more. I knew immediately that this was a pivotal point in our journey toward intimacy. It seems like there are emotional areas where Rhys doesn't want to venture. Yet, I want him to; perhaps even expect it at this point. Somehow, I have this feeling that together we have already passed the proverbial "point of no return" in our relationship.

When Rhys picked me up for lunch a short while later, I was able to go into more detail about my session with the therapist. He listened without the crusty emotional armor, and responded that he would do anything to help our relationship. I don't know why, but right now it feels like we just stepped on the yellow brick road; I'd be the one in the ruby slippers. Now if I can just find the energy to click my damn heels three times....

June 5, 2007

In two days my son will be walking in his high school graduation ceremony. Rhys and he are still very tight these days and Eli is expecting Rhys to be there for the big night.

Unfortunately, things don't always go so smoothly in this transition. It seems odd to think that being transgender would have any interference in a simple high school graduation, but it does. Rhys came to me and told me that just thinking about being at the ceremony gives him extreme anxiety. He doesn't want to be confronted with the chance of running into someone who met him in his previous body. Also, the suburbs where my son grew up mostly aren't exactly an open and welcoming community to trans people or issues. The average suburbanite would probably define "trans" as a car their dad drove in the 70s. Not a lot of diversity training is going on in Mr. Roger's neighborhood. What's difficult for me is being sensitive to Rhys' needs, supporting my son, and taking care of my own emotional self all at the same time. Being the adult child of an alcoholic I'm a professional at staying hyper aware of everyone else's needs, but not so much my own. I told Rhys that my first concern was his wellbeing, including emotionally. Hell, I've done ninety percent of my son's twelve-year education career with little to no support from another parent, so this shouldn't be so difficult to do alone, right? Wrong! You don't know just what you're missing in any situation until you have had something to miss. Now that Rhys is in Eli's life I get to feel what it's like to have support in every parental situation. There will be a gaping hole in the bleacher seat next to me at the graduation that no one but Rhys can fill. He wants to be free from the past, yet my history can offer up the most terrifying versions of it for both of us.

June 7, 2007

I met today with Rhys' therapist for the second time. Rhys came along. On some level the experience was truly comical. Perhaps being in therapy together isn't the most productive route, and yet definitely entertaining for me. When Rhys is with his therapist he behaves like a little four-year-old. A four-year-old in trouble. Theirs is a long-standing relationship and perhaps a somewhat parental one for Rhys in a good way. This woman has a way of instantly making any maternally orphaned adult wish that she was your mother. She is nurturing and validating but will simultaneously call you on your shit as soon as you try and dish it out. After hearing about her for years it was insightful to be in the presence of her and Rhys together. During the course of our conversation she pointed out several key things I need to remember:

1. My fiancée is biologically 43-years-old with an 18-year-old level of maturity. This explains a lot. Our tendency in arguing has become a roundabout with no apparent exit. His newfound fascination with certain parts of my body, moreover, border on obnoxious at times. If *only* I could remember these things in my greatest moments of frustration. Then perhaps I would find the humor before it was too late.

2. Rhys needs to take accountability for his testosterone levels. The doctor isn't monitoring his progress as closely as in the beginning and Rhys has taken it upon himself to increase the dose. The therapist reminded him that he needs to follow the protocol even if he doesn't want to.

Overall the session was beneficial and helped us to appreciate the ironic amusement of our situation. I felt bonded as we walked back to the car, my hand in his.

CHAPTER 8
But What Am I?

June 23, 2007

As I APPROACHED A BOOTH where Rhys was working for transgender health at the Gay Pride Festival, a young woman who had been in conversation with the group turned and started walking over to me.

"SO, are you *straight* then?" she demanded. *Come again?*

I responded in as reserved a voice as possible without laughing, "I'm sorry, but I don't know you."

Perhaps it was in that moment that she realized how inappropriate her question was coming from a complete stranger. On the other hand, just about nothing would surprise me at this point in our transition journey. She went on in an exasperated tone and explained to me that she has always identified herself as a lesbian. That was until her present partner came out to her as a transgender man. I glanced over at Rhys to look for a clue as to how this young woman had come to stand in front of me with all these questions. He shrugged his shoulders in innocence but my intuition told me he knew more than he was letting on at the moment. No worries, I would get to him later.

Meanwhile back to this confused young female standing before me.

"Do you base your sexual identity on who you are dating?" I gently inquired. She pondered my question,

"Well" she said, "I guess not, but I thought I was a lesbian. Now it turns out I'm seeing a guy and I don't even know what to tell all my friends and family anymore. My lesbian friends think I'm a sellout for seeing this trans guy, but I have really strong feelings for him and I'm just *so* confused!" she stated honestly. "You see" she continued "when we first got together he thought he was a lesbian too. Now that he has come out as transgender I don't know what to think." The pain was so evident in her young face and I felt immediately inadequate to be handing out trans-lover advice even at this stage in the process.

"Well," I began, "I can tell you this much about myself. As far as sexual identity goes I identify as queer. Part of this comes from being with Rhys over the last four and a half years. I am not queer because I am with Rhys and he is transgender. I am queer because I feel I could be in love with any individual, regardless of gender or sexual orientation."

WHOA. *Did that statement of confidence just come out of my confused head?* Perhaps I'll be okay after all. What's really beautiful is that each time I'm given an opportunity to explain or defend my relationship with Rhys, it brings about a clarity for myself that I didn't previously have. This young woman desperately wanted me to give her a magic answer to her own questions of sexual identity, yet I knew that giving her any such thing would be a lie. In this situation I deferred to my role as the parent of my two adult children. I tried to convey to her the confidence that her answers are only for her to find.

June 26, 2007

Twilight Zone, episode number...too many to count. As I have previously mentioned, Rhys and I are planning to get legally married this September. That was until the other day when our devious minds cooked up an even better scheme. We elope now without telling anyone and still have the ceremony in the fall. Our goal of intimacy will be met in a ceremony just for two. So today we hauled our butts, yet again, down to the courthouse with the intent to file for a marriage license. We got a number, filled out a form, and waited to be called up to the service desk. Rhys was nervous as hell. He can't seem to shake the feeling that he is perpetually deviant in one form or another. It *is* rather nerve racking though for us to go into these types of scenarios and wonder if we will get "found out". My worst nightmare would be standing there with the clerk and having them trip some sort of secret alarm under their counter because they have stumbled upon Rhys' former identity. All of the sudden a red light with a siren pops out of the recesses of the ceiling and we are officially busted. I wonder if they have a special booking code downtown for "gender deviants."

When our number was called out we headed to the counter and handed the application along with our driver's licenses to the well-groomed man waiting for us there. A few taps of his computer keys later we were handed a marriage license, and all the other paperwork required for our officiant to make it legal. We were wished good luck and sent on our merry way. Rhys waited until we were safely outside of the courthouse to let out his jubilation.

"We did it!" he hollered, "We got away with it!"

Can you imagine partaking in a legal civil right and believing you "got away with it"? This is precisely how marginalized we are as a transgender couple. I have to admit that at this point in time there is a small nagging fear inside of me that this marriage could be taken away from us if we don't fly under the radar. I don't even know if this could legally happen, but I sure as hell am not going to ask anybody either. What *they* don't know can't hurt *us*!

July 1, 2007

This afternoon Rhys and I walked into the woods at a state park and got married beneath the green canopy of the protective trees. We were in the loving embrace of a few close and supporting friends. There was a sense of irony around us that goes even further than the obvious transgender issue. Our dear friend who officiated the ceremony has herself been in a committed lesbian relationship for 14 years. The three people who were there to witness our vows were either transgender, gay or queer identified. So there we all were, gathered to experience a ceremony that, in 2007, is not legally allowed to two of the four couples present. In other words, a lesbian can marry us but lesbians can't get married. At least not at this time in the history of our "great" republic. Go figure. There are too many injustices to count in this situation.

I've wondered: How can I partake of this "right" without feeling some sense of remorse? This thought is one I have wrestled with for the past couple months. I want to be married to Rhys (and to gain the hundreds of state and federal privileges that brings), yet I don't want to further a law that excludes any other couple from achieving the same goal. I heard that Brad Pitt was quoted as boldly saying that he won't get married until that human right is allowed equally to everyone. I gave this a lot of thought and attempted to apply it to my own life. I fear not having the legal right to make decisions with Rhys in the face of all that is physically required to transition. I am mortified by the stories of same sex couples who are not allowed into a hospital room when their partner has been injured or becomes ill. I fear that if Rhys were in a serious accident I would have no right to speak for him if he couldn't do so himself. I am actually really afraid when it comes to this issue. I've read the stories of couples in the gay community whose partnership is worth nothing when the medical community becomes involved.

So for me, the ceremony represented a privilege and a right that has been hard-earned. In other words, our right to legally marry has come with a hefty price. After much heartfelt conversation and consideration we decided to legally marry. To stand up and take the privilege for ourselves, despite other couples being denied that same civil right. It was important to us in the face of injustice to speak loudly because you can. In addition, we pledged to educate by sharing the irony of our own story with others and to be strong advocates for marriage equality. No government has the right to tell its citizens when or whom to love. The only queer people are those who don't love anybody.

August 17, 2007

Last night Rhys said to me, "I don't really like to cuddle anymore." He may or may not have noticed my valiant and painful effort to hold back the tears and emotion that his few words brought. Yet another place of loss. Another time when my confusion over what is appropriate to share, becomes my decision to share nothing at all. Rhys' raw vulnerability with me concerning his changing physical body requires my utmost gentleness with his process. I take a breath and remind myself that this is just one moment, that things are constantly fluid…changing. Afterwards however, I can see only my own pain and loss. I am acutely aware of my growing desire to be held in direct correlation to his new found irritation with touch. Where to go from here? I have no idea. I want and need the physical connection we had prior to his most recent comment about cuddling; yet, I know the only person I can change is me. At this point I am finding it difficult to remain in the present moment: to refrain from projecting to five years out from now and wondering what it might be like: a daily peck on the lips from my incredibly "masculine" husband? I hope it won't be like that.

Recently a couple we know who are also going through the FTM transition together, visited with us. The female partner confided in me that they are struggling in their relationship. She said that her partner is having new feelings of attraction toward men. I felt her pain and panic all at the same time as I was able to remind myself that Rhys has never had sexual attraction to the male body.

I brought this whole topic up to Rhys and he told me that there was a time when he ventured there in his mind but was immediately turned off by the thought of it. Perhaps this is a more common occurrence than anyone in the FTM community is talking about. The one time I recall a public forum that addressed FTM sexuality was a reading of a play we attended called "Standards of Care." There were some dialogues of sex scenes acted out under a blanket on the stage that were so incredibly raw and poignant that both Rhys and I cried. Ironic, since the topics covered that night were ones we have rarely ever discussed or touched on. Yet there we both were, tears running down our cheeks.

August 21, 2007

Sometimes, I just sit and imagine his penis. I let my mind go to places that in the not so distant past would have been categorized as taboo for this ex-suburban housewife. I admit I actually enjoy doing this…A LOT. Why? Well, because the better I can visualize his cock while I am by myself, the more readily available that visual is when he is near. So tonight I went out on a limb and actually told him that I do this. Visualize dick, that is. Turns out not to be the same experience for him. He said it's all loss for him. There is a divide that exists between us that can in no way be crossed in either direction. We can listen, acknowledge, validate and empathize—and we do!— but never do either of us truly delve into the full process of the other. To be honest, this sometimes sucks. Because there are times (tonight for instance) when I want so badly to have him understand with exact clarity the feelings that I try and tell him through my words. But that's the trouble with perception: It relies heavily on the experience of the other person. So we talked less about *his* cock and more just about cock in general.

August 30, 2007

There was a time in the recent past when my journaling about our experience through this transition (these *trans*itions?), was beneficial to both of us. It has however become less and less likely for me to bring my new writings to Rhys for story time. I believe this is because I am becoming rawer with my own truth around all these experi- ences. This next spewing will most likely fall into that category of too raw to share.

Lately, I've been wondering: *Where did that guy go who pulled the car over at the sight of my bare knee, the man who dropped anything and everything to satisfy his own desires and my own?* These changes have crept in like smoke lingering in a room. So I decided to ask Rhys, "WHY?"

He answered in an open, vulnerable tone, "Because sometimes it's just *too* difficult. Being intimate with you triggers all my pain in being transgender. And sometimes that is more painful than others."

His response, so blatantly honest with not a trace of defensiveness, caught me in an emotional chasm. I looked at his soft expression and I immediately began to bawl. "That is so sad" I said.

SAD. Sad for him. Sad for me. Sad for us. So now I begin to understand the toll this transition plays on our previously ravenous sex life. In this moment this painful impasse is where he is. He loves being physical with me, but just as in every relationship, being physical calls for a risk of vulnerability. If this were a skilled game of chess, that move would be called "check." I have nowhere to turn with this information. You see, I want to know that "it isn't just me" but to find out what "it" truly "is." Here is this man, this person who with every day becomes more the man he has always intended to be. And with that knowingness comes an outward attractiveness which demands my attention. What I am trying to say here is that as he gets sexier and sexier.

"Over here, over here, look at me!" Truth be told, I am scared shitless at what the future brings for this area of our relationship.

Two weeks from Saturday we are having a wedding ceremony and celebration. Acting out for our friends and family the vows we secretly took over two months ago. I am in this…fully. I try to remind myself on a slightly irregular basis that this is just another point in the process. Nothing yet can be nailed down as permanent. Nothing. This thought process does help. At times. But then, sometimes not. Like now, as I sit here writing what I wish I could be telling him, hoping the response would be what we once shared. This feels dark. And from where I sit right now I doubt if it will be shared with anyone but me.

September 16, 2007

Yesterday I married Rhys (again). Fifty people gathered with us to celebrate our "right" to be legally married. He was dashing, and I felt every bit the blushing bride. My children wrote and read a beautiful blessing, and friends shared statements regarding our belief in marriage equality. Each person present was given the opportunity to submit a petition for marriage equality in our country. I counted them this morning. There were fifty.

Rhys' mother and two of his eleven siblings came to the ceremony. My family of origin was not invited. As I stood in front of fifty people who love, support and believe in us, I felt I was part of a much larger family. They reflected back their love for us, and I was immersed in a feeling of complete belonging.

The day was filled with reflection for me. Rhys and I have come a long way in his quest to become the man he has always known himself to be. Bittersweet as it was (looking out at our friends and seeing couples who are not allowed this same, basic right), I looked at Rhys and I knew that I was making the right decision for myself. This one man fills me with more joy than I thought possible for myself. His journey is the truest thing I have ever participated in with another person, and for that privilege, I would like to thank him. Rhys, my love, you define the word *soul*.

October 13, 2007

Yesterday, I gave Rhys his testosterone shot, and today he reminds me of how much of an asshole he is capable of being. I am not in a good place to bring this up to him, because he feels I unfairly judge him and blame the hormones whenever anything goes wrong in our relationship. What I know for sure is that his level of understanding and trust in me has sometimes gone backwards instead of forward in this process. Here is a femme biased description of the day after a testosterone shot: Any question before coffee is cut off with, "I'm still waking up!" Any trip in his truck is met with, "Look at that, look at that! Did you see what that idiot just did?!?!" And any innocent little question is met with, "So many questions!!!" Distance is the key here, as are naps.

October 18, 2007

Pre-transition: SEX, FOOD, NAPS. During transition: NAPS, FOOD, SEX. The beautiful mysteries of testosterone. Rhys is incredibly tired so much of the time. He is scheduled to see the doctor on November 29th and he intends to schedule his next surgical procedure (or as he so eloquently calls it, "having his organs yanked"). We are hoping that this will take place sometime during the holiday season. Rhys wants the doctor to save the organs in a jar so he can actually see them. There go my chances to top any other Christmas gift. After all, ovaries in a jar are pretty over the top if you know what I mean!! We can only hope that by removing these pesky little inhibitors, Rhys' body and specifically his hormonal function, will balance itself.

October 29, 2007

Today we had an appointment with the doctor to schedule Rhys' upcoming surgery. She explained in detail the many different procedures available for hysterectomy, then went on to urge the one she most prefers. Turns out she learned a new technique for performing the operation, just this past summer. She said that she really wanted to learn this for her FTM transgender patients. Apparently, Rhys will be knocked out, tilted upside down on an operating table, and the whole thing will be done laparoscopically.

Hmmm...

I guess my initial response of, "No way in hell are you going to hang him upside down and cut his belly" bordered a little on the overprotective. I'm extremely intimidated by the relinquishment of privacy and control his upcoming surgery will require of me. I feel better knowing that we are legally married, and that should I be required I will be granted the entitlement to make decisions on his behalf. But it's not only that. I hate that he has to be cut open, yet again.

Not the same for Rhys though. He can't wait to do this. The way he acts about it you would think he was getting a trip to the North Pole to visit Santa Claus. Rhys has an amazing ability to stay in the positive every time he is confronted with a medical procedure. He has been talking about and visualizing his recovery time for weeks now. Despite being told that he will need up to six weeks before he will be back to work, he defiantly states, "I'm taking one week off, and then I'll be healed and back to work."

It is not just a statement, but a mantra that he repeats many times a day. He amazes me. In fact, he chooses not to be exposed to any negativity around his upcoming hospital stay. This rule would also apply to me. In light of his request, I challenge myself to stay out of my fear and join him in the belief of his powerful ability to heal. I have been making an effort to push spinach on him every day, and we're eating healthy, balanced meals in preparation for the surgery. It definitely worked when Rhys had chest reconstruction. He was recovered and back at life within two weeks' time.

November 9, 2007

This morning we embarked on a journey to the suburbs, a place I rarely risk going to. But we had a real purpose (and the best intentions), upon entering a Baptist church that pulls barbs from my past. Thank whoever that we weren't there for any type of religious gathering. Quite the contrary, we had been asked by a friend in our office building to sit on a panel at a marriage and family therapist seminar. We were asked to speak on issues regarding transgender people, and those in relationship with them. We definitely have that area covered. So we volunteered in the hopes of helping to educate those who can potentially benefit our growing community.

Rhys, myself, and a transgender woman sat at the front of a room facing twenty to thirty therapists. Our therapist friend and her coworker presented information on the growing population of trans identified individuals. As they stated statistics and facts, the attendees were quiet and attentive. At some point they opened the forum to questions for the panel, and hands popped up in the air faster than they could be acknowledged. I wasn't so nervous in the beginning, but as I realized I had no control over what they might ask I felt an inner panic. Rhys looked uncomfortable too, and I was suddenly second guessing our decision to participate. As quickly as that feeling registered I was already having a question directed to me by a young woman near the back.

"Can you tell us a little bit about your experience around getting professional help in your situation of being partnered with a transgender person?" she continued, "And has it been helpful to have a therapist involved in your process?"

I let out a small breath of relief. I can answer this one I thought, without divulging too much personal information.

"My experiences with the mental health community during this transition have been numerous and not always positive." I explained. "In the beginning, I was looking for a new therapist to work with because mine had opted for early retirement. My initial visit with the first therapist I contacted was very odd. It took about 20 minutes into the session for me to realize that this woman was so intrigued by Rhys and his being transgender that my own reasons for needing therapy seemed to quickly fade. As many attempts as I made to bring the conversation back to myself, the therapy session would inevitably lead back to Rhys."

"I was frustrated, and knew that this person was not a good fit for me due to her lack of ability to focus on *ME*, her actual client." I went on to list the litany of therapists that I personally interviewed, recalling how I became quickly adept at recognizing that their fascination with the transgender issue would be the demise of my personal goals. During the panel discussion I was actually asked by one woman if I would be open to bringing Rhys into a therapy session with me, just so she could meet him. Four or five "professionals" later, I was referred to a strong, compassionate woman who had the insight I was seeking. I have been working with her ever since.

Another hand went up, "What made this therapist different from all the others?" Good question.

I described my initial meeting with my current therapist: how she listened intently to all my history, not *just* being in love with a trans man. After each piece of history I vulnerably gave to her, she would reiterate how difficult that must have been for me. And then she said something to me that touched my heart in a way that no other professional had, "The relationship you're in with Rhys requires that you are careful not to put more emphasis on his being transgender, than on your own needs."

Our relationship was solidified in that single comment. Her ability to perceive that being with Rhys at times makes it even harder for me to work on my own issues was exactly what I needed.

As I glanced around, I was aware that many of the therapists in this workshop were taking notes as I talked. Rhys was holding my hand, smiling next to me. In that moment I knew the importance of our participation on this panel. Here before us was an interested audience of mental health professionals, obviously intent on learning how to better assist the transgender community. I suddenly felt honored to be participating. As the Q & A session continued, my sense of nervousness quickly melted away with each respectful question asked by the participants.

In the evening as Rhys and I sat for dinner together, we had so much to discuss. It's amazing the way putting ourselves into new situations regarding transgender issues opens avenues of discussion we hadn't ever thought of. As we relived the morning, it became apparent how important these opportunities are in our experience. The more we talk, the more connected we are. Right now that's the key.

November 17, 2007

This was odd. I ran into a man from my past. A gay man. Four years ago we met up (after not seeing each other for a number of years), and I came out to him. At the time I was interested in a female-bodied Rhys. Today I ran into him at a neighborhood grocery store. I introduced Rhys as my husband. It may have been my imagination but it seemed that his face had a look of complete perplexity. I could almost read his mind…

Wait a minute, I thought she was on our side, how could she have gone and married a straight man? Oh, don't tell me she is one of those homosexual experimenters?

It's totally unfair and judgmental (not to mention insecure and short sighted), on my part to jump to such conclusions. Honestly though, I had this incredible need to justify my relationship with Rhys, born of the shame of being *perceived as straight*. How could these feelings be possible? I *am* the evolved woman who lets no relationship define her identity, right? Why do I care what another member of the LGBTQ community thinks of me? I was shocked and ashamed by my initial reaction to this awkward introduction. I guess the biggest thing I wanted was the validation and acceptance that was once there when the LGBTQ community recognized me as "one of their own." This relationship of being with a transgender person has come at a price. Rhys and I have, and continue to, struggle for our right to just be who we are. I do not want to identify as gay. And yet, a far worse scenario would be to have everyone assume that Rhys and I are the "average hetero couple." In that assumption a great portion of our experience is taken from us.

I felt shame about my strong urge to justify that Rhys is transgender and that I am still as evolved as the last time I saw this man. I guess my loss of community shows itself in ways I never could have imagined. I believe that through Rhys' transition I also have made some evolutions of self. Yet what I have felt today reminds me of how alone we feel in the "cover all" of the term LGBTQ. I refuse to give in to any remnant of my own phobias, in order to belong. So as we exchanged pleasantries, I let go of the urge to out myself to this man. After we were back at home I was relieved with my decision. I felt that if I had done any explaining to him about Rhys being trans, I would have felt emotionally naked. There is no need for casual acquaintances from my past to have verification of my continued identity as queer.

I'm happy I can name myself as queer now, as Rhys and I seem to be faced with more than our share of opportunities to reintroduce ourselves to our individual pasts.

November 18, 2007

Our Sunday afternoon movie date was interrupted by an unpleasant incident. We were about an hour or so into the film when an usher entered at the rear of the theatre. Rhys and I were sitting in the back row so we were the closest to him when he walked in. As we both turned to see what was happening, a large man walked behind our seats. As he passed he pointed to us, at which time the usher asked Rhys if he could please quit kicking the seat in front of him. Just at that time, the man who had initially complained demanded, "You got a problem with that?" in a very aggressive tone.

Rhys replied, "I didn't think I was kicking the seat, but you could have just asked me to stop instead of telling an usher."

The guy got really defensive, raising his voice and his accusations as he came at Rhys from behind. Rhys twisted in his seat and began to stand up. I could feel the recipe in the making for a physical confrontation. As the guy continued to accuse Rhys of being rude, I gently tugged on his sleeve and, in the attempt to be his voice of reason, reminded him that this fight wouldn't be worth it. The man stomped off angrily to his female companion on the other side of the theatre and barked at her, "Get up, because we are leaving!"

Where to begin? First of all, just to verify, Rhys was *not* kicking the seat at all during the entire time we were there. There was another young couple in the row directly in front of us who confirmed that they felt nothing the whole time. I guess everyone is entitled to their own perception of things (whether it matches mine or not!).

Secondly, it became obvious through his rude commands to the woman he was with that the accusing man was a very angry and controlling individual. But the most striking awareness that came out of this incident was that with Rhys' new and fully masculinized body come the repercussions of how some men deal with each other: "Back down or I'll hit you."

Seriously. As a woman this is something that never enters my mind as I stumble my way through this world. No doubt I am confronted with my own plethora of assholes who feel the need to patronize or sexualize me just because of my physical appearance. However, I can't imagine a lifestyle where the possibility of physical altercation is a real part of your daily reality. This man in the dark theatre was heavy, probably weighing in at least 275 pounds, and he was physically aggressive toward Rhys and me. For sure, *I* was not the one to be called to physical action had it gone to that. Ironically, the testosterone is working in unforeseen ways as Rhys had the instinct to protect me and then himself in that exact order. I find it fascinating that this is something that comes with the rugged terrain of being male. Some men will hit each other when and if they feel it necessary. I truly hope that Rhys is never required to act on this perplexing and powerful instinct. Undoubtedly, though, he would kick some ass.

November 19, 2007

As we've trudged through this swamp of inevitable changes, Rhys has made some recent improvements to our relationship. All that he said aloud was, "I am going to try and put aside my own insecurities so that we can have a better relationship." I can't wait to see what this means for me. Being as patient as this transition would require any partner to be is exhausting at times. But statements like the one he just made are the prize in the end. This simply reminds me that we are never in a place of permanence in regard to growth. In that knowledge lies the hope required for me to move forward with him. It's been two years of this transitioning journey, and even though I'm tired, he isn't done. I love him in part for the attribute of accountability to our relationship. The other part is simply this: I adore him.

December 2, 2007

Lately Rhys has been struggling with a foggy depression. He attempts, and often succeeds to stay just on the edge of depression's gaping, black hole, by exercising, taking vitamins and eating healthy. However, the magnitude of this crater is one that will not be ignored. These bouts of depression are concerning because trans people have a high rate of suicide. I can't help but be scared by it.

A few weeks ago Rhys decided to find a new AA (alcoholics anonymous) meeting in our area. During much of this transition, he has not been attending meetings because all the places he went prior for this support were women-centered. How ironic. So he has decided to test the waters of his newness.

"It was a success" he said after the first new meeting he attended. There was a great mix of people there, as we live in a very diverse part of Minneapolis. *But* there were no trans guys…only Rhys. A few men approached him and introduced themselves, including one gay man. He even gave Rhys his number and asked him to coffee.

When Rhys disclosed all this to me, he started to get emotional. He talked about how uncomfortable he felt in this setting of men. A feeling like he was still not "man enough" on the inside and might be found out. Yuck. What a terrible thing. I am sure these other guys could entirely care less about the man who is Rhys, sitting before them. Oh I don't mean to say that they don't care for him as a person, but that they aren't aware enough to scrutinize every person's individual presence to that extent. Regardless, it's still Rhys' own perception in these particular moments that creates the surge of insecurity. He said that he honestly isn't sure where he fits in society at this place in his transition. I'm sure if Rhys stood up in this AA meeting and announced not only being an alcoholic, but also transgender, he would be treated differently by some people for a myriad of their own reasons and insecurities. What Rhys described to me is that in everyday situations he finds himself often so keyed into how others see him, that he misses out on the content of life as it's unfolding before him.

December 7, 2007

There is this space between Rhys and me that I experience as a physical feeling. At times it's sharp and barbed, a place that if entered is guaranteed to cause injury. Yet that same exact space can quickly transform into the softest most comforting place I could ever imagine. Lately it shows itself as the former. I would describe this space as being the place where his edge and my edge meet. We all have boundaries in our relationships on one level or another (Let's hope). This space is where in our intimate relationship, he crosses over to me, and I to him. In the recent past this was a place for us that was more commonly visited than not. But as Rhys has gone further and further into the depressed disconnect between his mind and his present body, the space has become a place of confusion, and sometimes, pain.

Knowing what to do in these moments hasn't been my strong point lately. I say the wrong things, feel too much, expect something to happen, and on and on and on. I can't force him to feel anything for me, but more accurately I can't force him to feel anything *about himself*. He has entered into a quiet place in regard to his physical body. But it's so fucking quiet I think I just heard my own echo. I'm guessing the echo is offering me an opportunity to find new ways to communicate in our relationship. Lately, I've had this weird thought about what it would be like to be in a physical relationship with someone who has become suddenly and permanently paralyzed. It's my understanding that many of these relationships do not last due to the physical disconnect.

By no means are we in such a place of permanence. However Rhys' situation feels permanent to him. He tells me this. He will never be physically whole. This may sound hopeless, and yet it is as full of hope as the soul can reach. You see Rhys' realization that his body and mind will never be completely matched, is the beginning of an integration of self. He senses it happening right now. We talked more about the AA meetings and the anxiety and discomfort that go along with attending. As we sat across the table from each other, he said, "I think I can sense that you still feel *her* somewhere inside me."

As quiet, as still as I could possibly be, I listened.

Rhys went on, "It makes me realize how hard all this must be on you, because I have changed so much in this process. I am on so many levels, an entirely different person."

I could feel the sting of my tears as he added, "I know you must miss *her*, I can see it in your eyes."

OH.

MY.

GOD.

I dropped my head into my hands on the table and wept uncontrollably. I didn't want to cry. In fact, I didn't want to "do" anything. I wanted just to listen to him and be as fully present as I could possibly be. He read my thoughts and spoke them out loud. And when he put my feelings into his own words and recited them for me, I experienced a validation that covered me and was tucked under my chin like a blanket over a cold, tired child.

CHAPTER 9

Surgery, Yet Again

~~~

December 20, 2007

MERRY CHRISTMAS. Rhys is having laparoscopic surgery tomorrow. Hallelujah for medical advancements! He appears to be calmly prepared. I guess it would be understood on the level that you wouldn't miss a body part that you are entirely disassociated with in the first place, HUH? I however, am somewhat pensive about the whole thing. For one, have I mentioned that I have the wonderful knack for desiring control? Well it's true. Adult Children of Alcoholics can firmly back me on this. The other part is that Rhys' body is being handed over to "the process" at this time. As of tomorrow there will be a western medicine version of no holds barred. I will be spending the night at the hospital with Rhys as his appointed guardian of self-respect. Generally speaking, he is in impeccable health and this will be his first experience *ever* in a hospital. Even his chest reconstruction was done in a day surgery center. We are hoping to be introduced to a fully trans-enlightened staff, but one can never be too sure. Therefore, I have been given my instructions of care in case Rhys' drug induced recovery causes him to go "Jersey" on anyone who comes within ten feet of his body.

Today, Rhys was instructed to drink an entire gallon of electrolytes, aka "Go Lightly." Renamed by me as Go Heavily, it's designed to clear the bowels in a matter of a few hours after ingesting. Without getting too graphic here, mission accomplished. Now he can have nothing to eat for the next 24 hours. It's gonna be a long day.

December 21, 2007

The day has finally arrived. Rhys intends on spending his morning working, better he says, to keep his mind from obsessing about this afternoon's events. His acceptance of this surgery as his next step is a thing to behold. He proudly announced to me this morning that he shaved himself, belly on down. That way, he explained, there will be less messing with his unmentionables during his hospital adventure. We already lined up two friends to hang out with me at the hospital while Rhys is in surgery. Get this…they actually showed up late! For his surgery! I thought Rhys would blow a gasket before they got to our house he was so upset!

After arriving and parking we weren't inside for more than five minutes when the staff whisked him away. I was told that after he was admitted they would summon me on a beeper that I was handed. At that time, I would be allowed to sit with him while he waited for surgery. It truly seemed an eternity for that beeper to go off. When it finally did I was taken to the pre-op area to find my man swaddled in hospital gowns and robes. It was freezing in there. I found myself among the lucky who were actually clothed! He was so happy to see me. As I sat with him in the sterile whiteness, a nurse came in and inserted an IV line into his arm. Let the games begin! Unfortunately, the surgical team was running behind, and we were required to wait another hour. SIXTY MINUTES. What is it about that waiting thing? It's like the brain on drugs. The longer you have to wait, the more disturbing your thought patterns become. In this particular instance it felt torturous.

Eventually a nurse came in to get Rhys and I watched as he walked away with her down a tunnel of whiteness. He looked somewhat angelic with his big flowing robe open by his sides. He didn't turn around again. I wasn't sure what that meant, but I guessed that seeing me just wasn't what he needed as he rounded the corner into the operating room.

I was instructed to return to the family waiting area. Our friends were still there waiting for me. We hung out and read for the hour it took to for the surgery to be complete. Technology being what it is, there was a waiting room screen that was coded with numbers where I was able to check what stage of the surgical process Rhys was in. After we could verify that he was out of surgery, our friends took off and I continued to wait until Rhys was brought to a room. I don't recall how much time passed when again, my buzzer went off. All I can tell you is how excited I was to see Rhys. These moments waiting for him during his various surgeries have aged me. I mean permanently. And I am completely serious about this. I actually got to his room before he did, so I was there when they wheeled him in on a gurney. He was somewhat aware that I was there and managed a smile. I kissed him and his breath smelled metallic. But he appeared to be in one piece, although high as a kite. He managed to utter that he felt okay, just very tired.

The rest of the day was entirely uneventful, save one small but very important detail. There was a nurse. She was on the first shift after Rhys arrived in his room and she was from Somalia (I asked). From the time she walked into the room, both Rhys and I were aware of her discomfort with being assigned to care for him. I don't know what type of training these staff members are required to learn about caring for the transgender patient. Whatever it is, if she had received training, she needs to take it over a few times. She was very obviously doing her best to not have to *touch* Rhys. This can be a difficult task for a nurse, but somehow she pretty much pulled it off. It made me feel physically ill. She took his temperature (gloved), administered milk of magnesia (gloved), and then left the room without even a comment. In her speedy attempt to depart she left his hospital bed elevated. *Like four-feet up elevated.* This would be a job-costing faux pas in most hospital settings. As I lowered his bed, I made a mental note to discuss this with the doctor.

"That's okay," I wanted to say to her, "We don't need you or your judgment, I can take care of this man myself."

In retrospect, I have a sneaking suspicion there were cultural and religious beliefs that came into play here: beliefs that kept her from giving Rhys the same care that she would any other patient.

December 22, 2007

I attempted to spend the night sleeping on the "lounge chair" next to Rhys' bed. It was a long night for me. Not for Rhys though, he had the pain drugs. He slept except for when he was woken by the staff to be checked and monitored. When we woke this morning all he could think of was that I had brought homemade chicken noodle soup for him to eat. There was a kitchen for family around the corner from his room, and I was able to heat soup for him every couple hours.

He immediately wanted out of there. Really bad. But you probably know the routine; you wait and wait for the doctor to come in and give you permission to go home. After Rhys' surgeon came in for a brief chat, she gave him the news he was waiting for,

"As soon as you can pee on your own, you can go home!" There is no motivator like the word home when you're a patient in the hospital. Rhys was pissing like a pro and home in two hours.

He did well getting home and into his pajamas, now my job was to keep him down for a few days. I already had devised a plan to use Christmas cookies as leverage. It works every time.

December 31, 2007

Up to now Rhys' recovery has gone as he had visualized. He has been resting through the holidays and using his recent surgery as an excuse to eat as many Christmas cookies as possible. But last night was a rough one. Rhys woke up in severe pain and begrudgingly decided to give in and take a pain pill. I wished I could take one too!! He got so sick for a few minutes that I almost fainted. That would be just great. Him needing care and me passed out cold on the floor. Beautiful. His face was the pallid color of a sheet and pain induced nausea had overtaken his entire posture. In other words, he felt like total shit. Since narcotics take about twenty minutes to enter the bloodstream, there was no path to instant relief. I stayed next to him and rubbed his feet and legs as I became increasingly worried about what could possibly have brought this on. In addition to the pain, Rhys is getting more depressed with each passing day. He told me that he feels incredibly sad. He can't seem to shake it or figure out where it's coming from. I try not to think too much about all the unknowns in this process, but it's hard not to sometimes. I want to know what he is going through.

We spent the day hanging out at home. It was New Year's Eve and I was grateful for the holiday excuse. Since tomorrow is the first of the year and no one will be working, neither will we. Rhys has moments of feeling pretty good. But the last few nights have been a reminder that his body has undergone significant trauma. I swear to God that I'm gonna keep my mouth shut. Even if it drives me insane.

January 9, 2008

You know that saying, "What you don't know can't hurt you?" Well, I believe sometimes what you don't know *can* inevitably knock you on your ass. Prior to surgery, Rhys was expecting and visualizing his physical recovery. He had a mantra, "I'll be healed in two weeks," and it basically worked. He went back to work for a half day the Friday following his surgery; exactly one week to the day. Both Rhys and I are strong believers in the mind-body connection and its ability to expedite the physical healing process. But what of the mind-mind connection? What I'm trying to say here is: how do we heal our emotional selves when the pain is also intangible and sometimes equally elusive? Nothing was said about depression by anyone in the medical system who cared for Rhys. All the pre-op talk was about poop, pee, pain and limitations. I don't recall the doctor saying, "Now Rhys, you may experience some emotional ups and downs while your body is realigning its hormonal balance." I think if doctors talked to their trans patients, they would be better prepared to handle the emotional roller-coaster after surgery.

So here's Rhys, over three weeks postop and so profoundly sad that there are days where he wishes he didn't have to leave the house. At first it was somewhat vague as to what exactly was going on. Living through the Minneapolis winter can be an instigator of immense sadness in anyone. We even have a diagnosis for it up here: Seasonal Affective Disorder. Until you've spent ninety days in which the day is divided between 8 hours of gray and 16 of dark, you would be hard-pressed to understand how insidiously depression can creep over you. It's definitely not as dark as Alaska, but it still can suck. As time following the surgery passed, I became slowly aware that Rhys' sadness went much deeper than the doldrums of a sun-deprived individual. He talks about it to me here and there. I am very careful with his emotions right now. He seems extremely vulnerable.

So what exactly is going on in his body right now? I know for a fact he doesn't actually miss the organs that were removed. They were the last vestige of his internal female self, and to that he said good riddance a long, long, time ago. No, there is something harder to explain going on here. When he first started injecting testosterone, we learned that it would repress the production of estrogen in his body. Just prior to this last surgery he was told by his doctor that all of those hormones were close to gone anyway, so there wouldn't be much change. But here we are postop, and he is experiencing these undeniable hormonal changes. His night sweats are more intense than ever before and the lack of sleep only feeds his depression.

I feel incredibly inadequate and entirely helpless in this situation. I can be there and just listen; yet, there seems to be a greater need that has yet to be discovered or understood by me. With this surgery, an increasing distance between his comfort level with how his physical body presents male and what he feels about himself inside has become evident. It's not at all what I was expecting. I thought every step forward toward Rhys' fully transitioning would be to a better place. This part of *his* process has made this part of *my* process incredibly hard. I try to consciously remind myself on a regular basis that this place we are in isn't about me, or my level of attractiveness. Yet, at times I can go to a place of insecurity without even realizing it.

I was talking with a friend today and she was sharing how difficult it's been dealing with her mother's increasing decline from Multiple Sclerosis. She talked about how lately her mom has begun to choke and yet refuses to relinquish her right to eat solids (versus being entirely tube fed). Her mom has nearly choked to death on numerous occasions, often during family dinners. My friend said she is just beginning to understand that even though it is her mother who is experiencing the physicality of the disease, she too is having an experience, simultaneous and separate from her mom's painful, yet valid experience. With this realization she told me a friend gave her some advice. What she learned is that no longer is this disease just about her mother, but about the entire care-giving community surrounding her: family, friends and healthcare professionals.

I could see the parallels between our experiences and feelings. I cannot (and do not) compare Rhys' being transgender to any type of debilitating disease. I am merely making a connection between her experience and my own. I understand what it's like to stand back and let Rhys' needs take precedence. His experience of being transgender requires attention from both of us. Yet there comes a time (or many) where I am so profoundly affected by what he is experiencing that the experience becomes my own. I'm now trying to understand when and where it is appropriate for me to assert MY NEEDS based on this experience.

Needs? What *do* I need?

The Million Dollar Question....

I need to understand. I need to have boundaries. I need to know that eventually he will get whatever help is required (physically and emotionally). I need to know that he understands how this affects me. That it *does* affect me.

I need hope.

I need to be touched.

I need to be.

I need.

January 10, 2008

Yesterday, with the help of my therapist, I began to get honest about an emotion that has eluded me for most of my 44 years. I have to whisper it so no one will know I said it: It's...anger... Not only have I suppressed these feelings for most of my entire personal history, but yesterday I began to realize (and to give myself permission to have) the anger I feel around Rhys being born transgender. Right away I feel the need to explain, to justify how I could possibly have such feelings when ironically his *being* trans is exactly what attracted me to him in the first place. Yet I have no explanation. I'm as confused as my thoughts sound. I just know that he is sad, and that I can't help him. So I'm pissed.

The last few weeks have unfolded a thick blanket of depression and laid it gently yet firmly over Rhys. I'm beginning to feel like I can't find him anymore, even when he is two cushions over from me on the couch. His sadness has seeped into and temporarily filled all the places that once contained joy for him.

Last night we were talking in bed and I told him there are feelings that I intend to be working on now, things deep inside of me that need…deserve…to be shown in my character. I asked when would be a good time for me to tell him some of what I am going through. I wasn't expecting his response, "How about now?"

So I started talking. I told him what I know about my history with anger: my explosive and physically violent older brother, my father giving my mother the silent treatment, and the general taboo nature of me ever being allowed to explore this emotion at all. I explained how I feel out of control and confused when this emotion makes itself known, and how I then hold it in by sitting very still and not uttering a word. A virtual ticking time bomb. These patterns have not served me well and I need to break the proverbial chain. Why now? Very simply because this relationship I have with Rhys requires a level of honesty with me that prior to Rhys, I hadn't even known was possible. I went on to explain how my therapist asked me (and very persistently might I add), "Are you angry at the situation of Rhys being transgender?"

An immediate and conditioned "NO!" welled up into my throat. When she prodded me further to name my emotions around the situation as it is right now, all I could come up with was frustration.

"What are you frustrated about?" she inquired further.

I looked around and reminded myself that no one but my therapist would ever hear what I had to say in response. I sat for a moment and got honest with myself. Maybe I am angry. Perhaps I am angry that my husband's greatest desire is for his body to be congruent with his spirit, his essence, his soul. Or maybe I am angry that his transition seems to have dramatically and cruelly interfered with the most intimate places in our relationship. And it could very well be that I have anger around how the emotional effect of this one thing, this "transgenderness" of the person I love, has affected every single area of his life in ways that can't ever be changed. OH SHIT, I guess I *am* angry!

The hard question for me is, now what? What do I do with this anger when it seems so unproductive in the situation at hand? The only action I can come up with at this point is to sit down here and write my guts out until I feel I've said enough.

CHAPTER 10
Healing

January 28, 2008

WE CONTINUE TO NAVIGATE thru the shrapnel of what we once were. We keep picking up the pieces of our former relationship and putting them back together in a different pattern. It now seems the only way through. I look at him—HIM!!—and openly, yet silently acknowledge for myself how much I miss HER. Previously I wouldn't have dared write this word, her. It felt like a betrayal of what Rhys is asking of me. But now I have come to realize the magnitude of effect this transition has had, not only on Rhys, but on me. I now allow myself the gift of this intangible grief that I experience, and the compassion to accept all the other feelings that come with it.

I've been wondering how different this life change could look if our binary gendered society made a place for us. A place of unconditional support. A place of acceptance. I fantasize all the time of being openly queer and Rhys being out to everyone as transgender. How freeing it would be not to have fear as part of our daily navigation tools. I have a great sense of community with our trans friends, but I yearn for a day when we can equally relate to and be understood by the non-trans community, too. Lately I feel like I'm always hiding on some level. In order to protect our privacy and out of respect to not "out" Rhys, I have passed on numerous opportunities to share the truth of my own experience. I don't know how the world would see me. After all, the question of the day once was, "If Rhys is transgender, then who or *what* are you?"

And the only answer that remains is, I am Ali.

I feel the desire to repel the labels; they do not fit my self-description. No one regularly asks me what I like to eat, what movies I prefer to watch or what kind of car makes my heart race (Lexus SC430 hardtop convertible, by the way). But we are constantly asked to define ourselves based on the person we are partnered with. If you met Rhys this afternoon for lunch and spent one hour face-to-face with him, you would probably have no clue that he is trans. You would look at him and judge him instead, for all the other superficial qualities that get in our way every day: How tall is he? Where did he go to college? How much money does he make? Is he bald? Is he fat? Is he HOT? Yet, if in that same meeting he ventured to be vulnerable enough to tell you he was born in a female body, no doubt your perception of him would dramatically change. Gender is a great dividing line in our society. We are programmed to believe from the time we are born that the difference between male and female lies between our thighs. Women on one side, men on the other. Everyone else, an oddity, or worse, condemned to being marginalized. I believe we limit our own evolution in this painful mistake.

February 14, 2008

A few months back I was invited by a great friend to join a women's book group. I have been attending the monthly meetings ever since. The women who are involved are dynamic, educated, and a whole lot of fun. Each month as we discuss the chosen book (and everything else that comes up), I feel more kin to these women. Recently we read a book written by a good friend of one of the members. It was so unique to be able to get a perspective on the author from a firsthand experience.

I can't help but wonder when and if I will ever come out in this new group of friends. There are few people with whom I really want to share all I have written here. Yet these women, I truly respect. So I'm thinking; *Who could be a better audience for my journal than my very own book group? RIGHT?* Here's the catch: Once again this decision is burdened with the choice to "out" my relationship with Rhys. I am by no means ashamed, merely protective. This situation presents itself more frequently as of late, and is obviously providing an opportunity for me to figure out just what the hell I plan to do. I want so much to be able to make a decision as each opportunity presents itself, yet in those moments my gut begins to wring itself of its own frustration. I guess if I were truly honest here I would have to admit there's a feeling that a piece of my freedom has been inadvertently taken away from me. I want to speak my truth about our relationship without affecting Rhys. I struggle to find a way to say "Yeah, I am Queer," without divulging Rhys' transgender identity. I want to be counted amongst the family of those in the LGBTQ community yet to also gain this group's support in my admission.

The heaviness of my quandary lies partly in the story of my own actual coming out as queer. It took 38 years, yet lasted for only three, because around that time Rhys announced his intent to transition and his desire to live in the world as male. POOF! It took me back to a quasi-hetero relationship. I loved the time I spent "out" in the world. Those three years. I felt like I had earned it. After living 38 years as an often confused woman in a monogamous heterosexual relationship, my openness to new possibilities opened me up to myself. Tons of self-discovery....

March 14, 2008

This afternoon I received a distressed sounding voicemail from one of Rhys' sisters out in New Jersey. I had just finished working, so I called her back immediately. She informed me of something that we were expecting; Rhys' father died earlier in the morning. His dad was 88 years old and in failing health. He was also entirely estranged from Rhys. None the less, when I went back into the office and broke the news to Rhys, he was clearly devastated. What ensued was a gamut of emotion that took him by complete surprise. The gist of it is now that his father is gone Rhys will never have the opportunity to have a relationship (or merely a conversation) with him, man-to-man. This revelation has stirred up so much pain for Rhys.

I know my role in these moments is to be a validating sounding board more than anything else.

I ache for him right now. He has always wanted to be acknowledged as a son by his own dad. He felt that need all of his life, but his father didn't allow it. Perhaps in the end it's harder when a death happens and your relationship with that person is unresolved. Harder even than if you had a wonderful, fulfilling bond. Here's yet another place where Rhys' transgender identity brings up loss. The intangible loss of never being acknowledged as his father's son.

March 25, 2008

And suddenly we are in New Jersey, attempting to sort through the remains of what was once Rhys' childhood home. Since his father died, the decision has been made that his mother cannot live alone in the house where she lived with his dad their last forty-odd years. What we came upon as we arrived here was the realization that nothing has been thrown away from this house in at *least* forty years. Rhys' sister, nephew and the two of us set about the daunting task of emptying out the contents of the entire house.

On the second day, I went upstairs to one of the bedrooms to tackle what at one time was Rhys' room. The remnants of a life lived were stacked waist-high from the door frame on in. I just started pulling things off the top of the pile and carrying them down the stairs for someone else to sort through. The process was like going backwards a decade at a time. On the top of the pile I found discarded toys and remnants of Christmases from the past 10 years or so. There was nothing too remarkable about the items that I was unearthing, except for their age. That was until I got to about knee-deep in the pile. It was at that place that I began to realize that what I was sifting through were the leftover pieces of Rhys' childhood. Artifacts of the 1960s and 1970s. I'm not exaggerating here. There were religious plaques with his female given name, boxes of pictures and clothes, and anything else you could imagine from a childhood bedroom. Once I was able to create a path, I made my way to the closet. There inside on the floor, I found a large wooden box with a lid. There was no one else with me upstairs and need I say that I was more than curious to know what I would find under that lid. I carefully lifted the dusty, quilted box out and brought it into the hallway, a space where I could actually find room enough to stand. I felt like stinkin' Nancy

Drew. There was a feeling in my chest like I was about to get into big trouble. But I didn't care, I was just too damn curious. Inside I found carefully stacked school notebooks, high school varsity letters and notes to friends...all with the same name on them. *HER* name. Before me lay Rhys' past, saved for over 30 years through the mere negligence of organization. His sister mentioned to me earlier that no one had even been in this room for 10 *years!*

As I sat with the box I didn't want to disturb the contents. I just stared at them with the lid open. Gently, I brushed the tips of my fingers over the papers with *her* handwriting. I ran my index finger over *her* name. I felt compassion toward these inanimate objects from *his* past. Somehow I was honoring *her* there, the life that *she* lived, the pieces *she* absently left behind. How ironic then that I should be the one to discover this personal history of the one I fell in love with. I so wish I could have known *her* then. I wanted to imagine myself playing in the back yard with *her* in 1973. All these thoughts and feelings came bursting out of me at the mere sight of her handwriting.

My awareness was abruptly brought back to the hallway, when I heard Rhys holler up the stairs in his tone of endearment, "What you doing up there Ali?"

"I'm coming right down!" I replied. But not before I had one more moment with the tangible, physical energy of *her* past.

The box was heavy, and as I lifted it down the stairs I said to Rhys, "I have something to show you."

"What is it?" he asked, uninterested. All day we had been unearthing, sorting through, and throwing out literally *tons* of possessions and garbage (in the end we filled three 12 ton dumpsters!) As I gently sat the box down on the dining room table, he showed no recognition. Then he opened the lid. As soon as he understood what I had found he seemed slightly embarrassed. Perhaps even agitated. He commented without really paying much attention to the contents, "I don't care about that stuff; just throw it."

"But sweetie your high school letters and stuff are in there, don't you want to look?" I asked. I felt protective of the young person who Rhys once was, confused, struggling and trying to make a way in this life.

"Here," he said as he picked up the box, "I'll take care of it." With that he headed out the front door, down to the curb, and threw the box into the gaping mouth of the thirty-foot dumpster out on the street.

I felt very still inside. I know he needed to do that for himself, and I am so glad that I did what I needed to do before I presented him with these relics from his past. The energy of what I touched was still in me, it felt sacred to me...the female person he once was.

April 1, 2008

Something really cool has been happening over the past few months. We're making new friends in the transgender community. Really good friends. Rhys met a guy and they had an instant bond of friendship before I even had the chance to be introduced. It seems that he and his wife have been living a somewhat parallel life to ours over the past three years. In fact, their stories are so similar to our own, it is uncanny. Which is why it's so effortless hanging out with them. There is no need for explaining the road we are traveling because all along they were in the car right next to us.

This friendship from the first introduction has entirely changed our lives. Rhys will find any reason possible to sneak off and hang out with his "buddy." For the very first time in the process of Rhys' transition, I am beginning to feel insulated by a strong community. Suddenly, we are receiving multiple invitations to parties and gatherings where trans and queer people are the majority population. And of course our cool new friends are always there as well. As time passes, I realize how important Rhys' new friendship is. He appears to be much more content in his own life as he spends time with the men who understand him the best...other trans men.

I am acknowledging for myself the extent of our isolation over the last two years. This, paired with my new awareness of the community growing around us, is again pointing out to me that this is a process of change. A short time ago I didn't even leave a space for the chance to find friends who are partners of trans guys. At times I have just felt so damn stuck.

Recently, I met a woman who is dating a guy that just came out to her as transgender. She told me that she was actually the catalyst in his revelation. When he came to her with his maleness, she was not at all taken aback. We've been getting together for coffee and she enlightens me with her ease. She seems to take each step of their journey in stride. In other words, she doesn't take personally the various transitioning trans faux pas. I have great gratitude for these "partners in crime" who have walked into my life. Gradually, I have opened myself to these relationships and it feels so good to walk away from a trans-talking session and know that I am safe in my vulnerability. As women, we are able to share the most taboo of transgender topics and get support for even the uncomfortable stuff. For example, "Hey, wait a minute, where the hell did my girlfriend go?!"

May 11, 2008

We just came off the rush of participating in the second annual trans health fair in our city. Both Rhys and I were teaching workshops over the weekend and had been anticipating this event for months. This was my very first opportunity to lead a topic on being the partner of a transgender person. My nervousness came largely from not being able to anticipate the type of crowd my workshop would attract. My intent was to address the topic of intangible grief for the partners in these relationships. Recently, my writing has brought me to realize that I'm still in pain around some of the things that have changed (disappeared) in this process. My fellow trans lovers have affirmed the same in their own stories. We all have this commonality except for one little detail; no one is actually *talking* about this. It seemed this would be as good a time as any (which by the way, there is no good time to talk about this stuff to a transitioning trans man), to breach this topic. Like I said, I had no idea what to expect in terms of numbers or group makeup, and kind of went into it thinking I would have to adjust my content depending on this.

As I waited in the assigned room with two friends in the community, I was aware of people kind of shyly peeking in the doorway. Eventually a few women trickled in, and as the circle of chairs began to fill it was like a sudden green light for whoever else had been lurking out in the hallway. There was standing room only and it was past time for us to begin. Initially, I wanted to know where the hell are all you people the other 364 days of the year? My god, there were so many "partner-identified" individuals in this room, I tried to inconspicu-ously count-out how many transgender people that would mean they are dating. (If they each are only dating one!) There was an energy of excitement and apprehension and I felt my mouth going dry in nervousness. This was all about my lead. I had brought excerpts from my journal, and was mortified at the mere thought of sharing these accounts of my own recent history.

"What if they don't relate?" I thought. "What if I say too much and am left here with my trans-loving heart, all on display and beating for everyone to see?"

I was aware of quick sideways glances between those around me. It has come to my attention that throughout this process it's not only the transgender individual who tends to put up a coat of armor in protection from the rest of the world. It's us too. Those of us who love the vulnerability of a trans person. We carefully monitor and choose each and every situation where it might possibly be safe to honestly share our story. I felt honored to be in this circle of support, and was intent on showing that integrity in every word I spoke. I began with introductions. Those who wanted to remain anonymous could pass, yet I felt the tension level rise in the small room. As the invisible toss went from one to another, each and every person daringly stated their name and why they decided to attend this workshop. The content of these introductions could have been a workshop in and of itself.

One woman who I had never seen before, declared "I'm Sophie, and I'm pissed. That's why I'm here today."

Shit...anything else you want to start with?

My fear of "lack of participation" melted away with each bold announcement of name and intent.

I began with my experiences of loss and anger and read from my journal excerpts. Afterwards, I opened the group to discussion and saw ten hands shoot up in the air with urgency. Stories were shared of male chauvinist comments made by testosterone inflated lovers. So many heads were nodding in acknowledgement I couldn't begin to imagine the experiences that could be shared amongst this group. Literally. One woman humbly related this story; "All of my adult life, I have considered myself a lesbian woman. So when my girlfriend (at the time) came to me and told me she was a trans guy, I was confused. However, I knew that I loved her, and that I would love him as well. Never have I been attracted to the male body and especially *not* the penis. I really didn't give it much thought because I knew I was attracted to the female form." She bravely continued, "But as he began to transition he became obsessed with the fact that he didn't have a penis, and he desperately wanted one. I was horrified and confused to find myself missing his penis as well. The fact that he wanted it so much and that the absence of this body part made him feel incomplete, made me want it for him. I was so confused and shocked by my feelings, I was questioning my own sexuality." I began to cry, witnessing her boldness.

She went on, "Then I thought a lot about it and came to peace with my confusion. I only want what he feels makes him whole, and even though I still think of myself as a lesbian, I wish I could make love to him in the physical way that he would desire. That would include the penis."

Her vulnerability brought similar feelings to the surface of the group. There followed a plethora of discussion regarding what to do about our partner's sexually changing bodies. Personally I have never before witnessed the kind of openness and raw emotion exhibited here, by the partners of trans men. Among the obvious feelings of loss, there were the occasional outbursts of anger. One woman told the group that she never intended on signing up to be with a man, but now that her lover had begun to transition she was too deeply in love with him to leave. She said she felt "duped."

As the hour went on, I realized there was a woman in attendance who wasn't a partner of a transgender person. She introduced herself as Morgan, and made clear that she was a therapist doing research for her doctoral thesis on partners of transgender men. I'm not exactly sure how the group members individually received this information. I was definitely intrigued. The workshop ended, and anyone interested was asked to leave their name and number with the therapist. I couldn't wait to talk to her. Anyone who wants to listen to my crazy trans partner rantings is cool by me! I signed on to five hours of recorded interviews in which I will be given open forum to discuss anything I wish about being with Rhys. YEEHAH!

May 23, 2008

I felt apprehension and excitement as I woke up this morning. Today was my first of five interviews with a therapist who is writing her thesis on partners of transgender men. I can honestly admit I had no expectations on the meeting, but at the same time wasn't sure how much of myself and our story I was willing to share. Thankfully, my unease was put to rest within the first ten minutes of meeting Morgan.

Her office was comfortable and private, and after I was asked to choose a seat she began to explain her interview process to me. Each session is to be recorded and anything said will be confidential, including the names of Rhys and myself. She explained that I had the power to stop the interview at any time and decline to answer any question she may ask of me. The first meeting would be comprised of a background interview. She had pages of specific questions relating to my past, and to the present relationship that I am in with Rhys. After this session however, the next four will be an open forum for me to discuss anything I wish around being with Rhys. Wow. Hard to believe that anyone truly wants to listen about this one topic for that long. We're talking *four hours* here! She doesn't have to twist my arm; I'll talk for 40 hours if she would like! No one else has given me their ear for four hours of trans talk…and I don't blame them. To the average listener this topic can become somewhat daunting. Even some of my closest friends don't always fully comprehend the gender vs. sexuality issue. It's one of those baselines of understanding that determine the depth of any conversation regarding my relationship with Rhys.

Morgan began by asking me about my experiences in my family of origin and then moved on through my life from there. She inquired about my parents, siblings, significant experiences and the environment in which I was raised. I talked about my previous relationship of 22 years. As she was asking and I was answering, I was listening to myself. What I heard was an amazing proclamation of truth. MY truth. I felt confident in most of my responses, and simultaneously astounded at that confidence. I realized how strongly I knew even as a teen that boys weren't the only ones catching my curious eye. I liked looking at the girls too. Especially the tomboys. Hmmm…? (How about the Rhysboys?)

An hour passed as though mere minutes and it was time to end, much sooner than I would have liked. I was paid twenty dollars for my participation and felt extremely awkward being compensated for the emotional cleansing that I had just experienced. I scheduled the next four interviews and left feeling less alone than I have in three years. Again, the validation was tangible and something I craved. She didn't need to say much in response to what I was sharing; the mere act of her listening made truth out of so many pieces of my story that I have never had the opportunity to share. As I walked out into the downtown Minneapolis sunshine, the streets blurred with the four o'clock retreat of the corporate masses. I lifted my eyes and whispered out loud to the blue sky, "Thank You."

May 26, 2008

The truly significant part about participating in these interviews is that it's opening a new forum for discussion between Rhys and me. When I came home the other day he wanted me to recall and share every single thing that was discussed between Morgan and me. As I explained an overview of the process, I realized that he was just the slightest bit envious that I was sharing so much about us...about ME...and that he wasn't a part of it. I can see where he might feel envious, but I felt somewhat guarded about all that I *wasn't* willing to tell him. The reason is simply this: the whole thing feels like it's mine. Finally, a place where I get to be the center of attention to purge the feelings and thoughts that aren't so pretty. Not only that, my thoughts and feelings are often times loud, sometimes angry, and always come with a slight flavor of guilt. It feels private and I realize I want it to stay that way. Not without some feelings of regret, after all there isn't much that Rhys and I haven't shared with each other over these past three years. What I have realized from just one hour of being interviewed is how deep my need is to have a place of my own to talk. And bitch. And cry.

So I shared with him what I thought would obviously comprise an hour of my time and deleted what I have yet to process on my own. Fair enough. He seemed satisfied with my explanations, as was I with the new awareness and openness I could see in Rhys. It's interesting to me how every time we bring a third party into the mix he is much more candid relating to his own feelings than when he and I attempt to navigate on our own. For whatever reason this may be, I am extremely grateful. I view these interviews as a golden opportunity for self-understanding, growth, and healing. And since Morgan is a therapist, yet not *my* therapist, there is an air of low-risk irresponsibility in it. When I attend therapy with my own therapist I go with a purpose. Within that purpose there is a responsibility of awareness. This situation however, feels freer. Morgan is simply there to gather information for her thesis, and I have no accountability to her other than to show up. Whatever else I decide to take from these interviews is entirely up to me. I like it. At times therapy and the consciousness it requires is more exhausting than the problems presented there. Sometimes it's just nice to emotionally vomit and then leave. No cleanup required.

June 7, 2008

Yesterday was the second day of the trans-lover interviewing process. And, Wow! Morgan's listening ear has allowed a crack to open in my soul, and the innards are oozing out. As I again sat and listened to myself speaking, I became aware of thoughts and feelings that up until now I have only allowed to fester in the silent regions of my soul. Morgan comes prepared to each meeting with dozens of inquiries that help tap into those dormant regions. She asked me earlier what made my relationship with my father so special. I explained how he was a quiet man: that he thought a lot and spoke little. He had a presence, and it was respected; a prescribed authority of sorts. It took patience to truly know my dad and I felt it was worth it. He was a research scientist and on the exterior presented as a left brained thinker, but he was truly an emotional soul-seeker. Morgan also asked me to describe myself, and in that self-portrayal I included that I am often pigeonholed out in public as a "straight suburban woman." Part of me really revels in the fact that I don't present physically the way society would expect, given my queer orientation. In other words, if you don't *know* me you *really* don't know me. (Which is perhaps true for everyone?)

As I was speaking to Morgan this afternoon she inquired about my attraction to Rhys. Ultimately, I have to say that at the top of my list is that when I met him he was a female-bodied person and yet was most often perceived as male. If you met Rhys back then you probably wouldn't have known what his gender/sexuality story was. Even now in his transition, I think the fact that he is transgender is hot...so hot that he is now identified as male and the majority of the world has no idea of his previous form. For me his being transgender is over-the-top sexy!!

It was at this point that Morgan brought about a light bulb moment for me. She said, "Wow, I find it really interesting that in describing your father, Rhys and yourself, you have pointed out a glaringly similar characteristic that you find attractive and valuable."

I couldn't wait for her to continue.

"You described your Father as being quiet and somewhat mysterious, that his external self and his internal self were two entirely different expressions. You stated the same about yourself, and then went on to describe your attraction to Rhys in parallelism to those previous descriptions." She went on, "It seems to me you have created a triangle between the three of you, have you ever noticed that?"

I was dumbfounded. I felt like I was going to cry. My dad died way too soon (at the age of 50), and I loved him so much. Ever since I have been with Rhys I have realized more and more how like my Father he is and I love it. These parts of Rhys feel familiar and comfortable. However, I have never taken it to the level of linking the three of us. It's so wild to unearth the core of my attractions to Rhys, and it's a gift for me to know that some piece of it is connected to the love I had and still have for my wonderful father.

I need time to digest everything we talked about, but one thing I know for sure is that my dad would be very happy with the love I have found with Rhys.

June 12, 2008

Rhys is very curious about what I say to Morgan. I am becoming increasingly brave about omitting most of it. As time is passing between these interview sessions, a sting of rawness has become an unwelcome companion. So much of what I am sharing with her has not been shared with Rhys up to this point. Probably for good reasons too. I can honestly admit that if I had allowed these things to surface early on in Rhys' transition, we more than likely would not be together as a couple. Rhys requires space to experience the physical transformation he has made over the last three years. More and more space was then taken as the physical process included an emotional component. I now realize that as his need for attention and validation grew, mine outwardly shrunk to allow that place for him. I'm not saying this was at all healthy; I'm just saying it was. These interviews have become a safe space for me to purge three years of emotion that have been inadvertently pushed aside. Can you believe I am actually being *paid* to participate? I intend to make the most of it. I'm still pretty confused about what and how much to share with Rhys regarding the grief and loss I have experienced during his transition. My hope is that this process will shed some light.

June 16, 2008

As hard as I try I can't refrain from reminiscing about the first three years we had together. It's not a very helpful practice, as it brings cause for second guessing me. In my unhealthier moments I wonder what *I've* done to bring about such a drastic change in our relationship. His process triggers my most insecure feelings, and my challenge is to try and remember that *before* I begin to rip myself apart physically for not being thin enough, sexy enough, smart enough, blah, blah, blah! A real mind fuck. There are times when I don't even have the energy left to visualize a future that includes Rhys feeling whole in his body. That sounds pretty apathetic, and truly I don't want to go down that road. This is a lonely place I'm in.

June 27, 2008

HAPPY PRIDE!! To think that only five years ago I attended my first pride festival. I remember I went with a friend at the time. An "out" lesbian with years of exposure in the gay community. She kept leading me forward through the crowd with her hand on my low (top of the ass?) back. I was then unaware that she wanted more than my friendship. Naivety? Denial?

I'll let you be the judge. Regardless, I was fresh meat any way you grind it.

Fast forward...2008. Rhys and I are now aware of every single trans related event during Pride weekend. We have many friends in the trans community, and have been invited to "trans pride" parties. We have come a long, long way. The reflection is good if only to remind me that Rhys will not be mis-gendered at any time in our future.

To kick off our weekend, we attended a showing of an independent film at the Walker Art Center. All weekend long there will be films relating to issues in the LGBTQ community. The auditorium was (disappointingly) only filled to about thirty percent, and we saw a few people we knew from the transgender community there. This evening's film presentation was titled, XXY. The film told the story of an early teen/child who was born intersexed. It appeared that the gender presentation of this child was predominantly female. Yet throughout the film, she/he experimented with all areas of gender. Her/his parents were very supportive and were searching for ways to make the transition from childhood into young adulthood easier on their child. Injections of anti-androgens were being given to her/him in order to repress the impending signs of male puberty. She/He was being encouraged by her parents to make a decision regarding which gender presentation would best fit her/his identity. The emotion in this film was painfully accurate.

As we watched I found myself thinking what it would have been like if one of my own children had been born intersexed. Imagine having to wait the years it would take for the child to realize their own gender identity. In the process, I think the teasing would border on torturous; children can be wickedly cruel to each other in regards to their differences. As a species we have a long way to go in our understanding the intersexed individual. I can't even fathom the protectiveness a parent would feel for such a child.

At some point, I looked over at Rhys in time to see a tear roll down his face. Which in turn got me to crying. As a couple we have discussed transgender issues for hours upon hours, and at times the direction of our conversation has taken us onto the idea of being born intersexed. I personally have only met a few adults who are out as such. Their experiences, growing up in a world that is completely unaccepting, are horrifying to me. I don't understand how as a culture we have taken such amazing strides in intellect and technology, yet seem stalled when it comes to gender diversity.

Films such as the one we saw this evening would be helpful in educating a population that is seemingly confined to binary gender roles. Unfortunately, it is often only those who are intersexed or genderqueer who show any interest in seeing such a film. I believe it would be brilliant to include films on gender and sexual diversity in the curriculum for high school seniors. To introduce the mere *idea* of having more than two options in expressing yourself would create a gender revolution! I wish that my own two children had been allowed this freedom in their educational experience. Independent films can at times be difficult to find outside of a theater environment, but with the Netflix generation has come thousands of opportunities to learn about subjects that were perhaps never before available to the general public. I strongly encourage everyone to try and see this film, and afterwards start talking about it in mixed company. See what happens.

July 24, 2008

During Pride last month, I ran into a woman in the trans community who I have spoken with a few different times throughout this journey. The first time we met was at the Forge Conference in Milwaukee. That was already a year and a half ago! Well you know what they say: time flies when your…husband just transitioned from female to male?!

Anyway…since that time we have had a few opportunities to update one another on the progress of our writing. What? You don't remember me mentioning that she is writing a book as well? Well let me refresh: This woman was awarded a grant to write on her experiences being with a transgender man, namely her husband. Yeah I know! What are the odds? Not only that - she practically lives in *our* neighborhood! This is for real. I wasn't threatened by her impending publication, merely intrigued. Besides, I can't be a critic of a piece of work I haven't even read.

Knock, Knock!

Who's that?

Oh, look, it's opportunity at my door!

Yesterday we attended a reading that featured this author and her new work. The event was being held by a local LGBTQ Reading Series and took place in a great little gallery down the street from our house. I wouldn't have missed it for the world. The place was packed and I was honestly so excited for her to have such a large, supportive audience. After all, she is writing about being with a trans-gender man. We trans partners need all the publicity we can get! She was an eloquent reader and what she wrote was the sterling truth. I think I should get to be the judge of it because believe me, if someone attempted to write bogus accounts of their experiences being with a trans guy, I would be able to sniff it out from a country mile! The courage and insight in what she wrote served as a bold reminder that each and every one of our stories is worthy of an audience. I have immense respect for this author, and cannot wait for her book to be published. I would be honored if she were to read what I have written here.

September 10, 2008

My life with Rhys now has become much more predictable than it was in the last three years. In some ways this is good and in others... well, I don't know. I definitely *do not* miss the rollercoaster ride that was our life out in public while he was transitioning. Gone are the days of an offensive, "Can I help you Ma'am?" No more running home in the middle of a meal just so he can take a piss. Many of the painful historical facts of his journey will permanently remain just that, the past.

The one thing that is guaranteed for all of eternity...

She,

is

never,

coming

back.

This one, undeniable fact requires me to take action. It is now me who needs to make the changes in our relationship. Of course I have been doing this in one small way or another over the past three years, but I am speaking here of permanent adaptations to the way I interact with Rhys. Knowing that I need to do this and actually following through? Two entirely different things.

What is my hesitation? Why would I not want to adapt to Rhys' amazing newness? The answer to these questions may not be as obvious to everyone else as they are to me. I know damn well what I'm holding back, and here it is in its simplicity:

Making these changes would require me to say good-bye *forever* to someone I have loved perfectly and completely...

Her.

November 7, 2008

I have entered a place where denial is no longer my friend in Rhys' transition. There are many truths that even six months ago I would have been happy not to know. First and foremost would be the awareness of his indelible changes. But coinciding with my daughter's recent relocation to the east coast and my son's daily gains toward independence, a chasm of space has opened in my life that once was occupied by their ever-pressing needs. What I am now clearly aware of is that this time has been presented to me as a gift of self- discovery. The quieter my life becomes, the louder my feelings scream at me, "Pay Attention, Woman!" It truly is amazing to me the range of self-denial that can occur over 20 years while mothering two children. Add to that, three years of Rhys transitioning.

While reading yet another self-help book (in my personal library of dozens), I was confronted by the unsettling realization that perhaps *I* am struggling with emotional insecurity. My first response (of course) to this awareness was, "Fuck that!" but I knew that such a charged reaction only meant I was being triggered in my most core emotional places. So I made a withdrawal from my newfound savings account of quiet time and meditated on this possibility.

Emotional insecurity?

The words alone are like a slap to my ears. No one really wants the word insecure attached to them in any way…especially me. So I dissected them in my head in an attempt to diminish the feeling of vomiting in my own mouth.

1. Emotional? Well, yes; I surely cannot deny that I am an emotional person. Born an intuitive Pisces and self-raised in a family where emotional (and physical) survival was the primary goal of each and every day. I have been aware for many years that my emotional self is highly sensitive and at times vulnerable.

2. Insecure? Well. How about not secure? Lacking security.

Okay… yeah! I can deal with that. So, lacking emotional security… Security to me defines a peaceful mode of survival. For the past six years of my life this has come in only very rare instances. The first three of those years I was running (literally and figuratively) at a pace of fight or flight. I was single and living alone for the first time in my entire life. I had two teenage children with all of their natural pubescent angst. My financial survival was completely dependent on my new small business, and I was concurrently attempting to purge the toxic emotional waste of my own childhood festering within. This narrative is possibly the antithesis of, "a peaceful mode of survival."

Prior to Rhys, my history of intimate relationships did not include *even one* that would remotely register as emotionally secure. I now realize that my feelings, even when expressed, were repeatedly invalidated. First as a child, then as a child bride. For years the message of emotional unworthiness grew at a rate not to be rivaled by my increasing level of resentment. As I began to create a new life for myself as a single woman, I struggled to digest all of the self-discovery that was coming my way. Along came Rhys. Mr. Validation himself. It was, ironically, his emotional gifts to me that only heightened my journey of emotional worthiness. So it is with irony that I realize the process of his transition has brought about a fresh, new batch of emotional insecurity in me. Let me further explain. In the beginning of our relationship, Rhys and I related to each other very differently than we do at this point in the process. How could we not? Even though he felt his gender expression was best represented as male, he was truly in the physical (hormones included) body of a female. He was altogether softer. This was Rhys on estrogen. All of these qualities have since changed. I don't make these statements as a right-to-wrong comparison; they are merely what they are. And through these changes I have experienced a mounting level of emotional insecurity.

Last night I shared these revelations with Rhys. He quietly listened to my newest self- awareness, and when I finished he replied, "Wow sweetie, that's some really deep stuff. It almost seems like you are with someone who has suffered some weird form of amnesia. Because, although I can listen to you talk about the way I was before all this and validate you, *I honestly don't remember most of it myself.*"

I explained to him how difficult it has been at times during these last three years, not to internalize the new way he relates to me.

Even though they cannot be medically named, some key pieces of his personality have undergone drastic changes. His devotion to me remains the same, but his expression of this is entirely different from when *he* was *she*. As I realize these deeper places of pain in myself, I am admitting (out loud) that it's okay to talk about the parts of our experience that maybe haven't seemed like progress. Because surely emotional insecurity can't be progress. But what I know for sure is that the potential for progress lies in my ability to be honest with myself, and then to look at these feelings in an attempt toward personal growth. This is my present intention.

CHAPTER 11

It All Comes Down To This...

~~~

November 26, 2008

RHYS AND I CURRENTLY NAVIGATE through this world together on the exterior, similarly as any other couple. It is now only the vast and various terrain of the *interior* that separates us from the world of the gender binary. Following the last surgery, Rhys somehow miraculously moved out of his most recent depression. It was such a gradual change that I only realized in the past few days that overall, he is feeling really good. He talks quite a bit about the next surgeries and how desperately he wants to have them. Waiting seems like a ticking time bomb inside Rhys. Yet, he also acknowledges that the seventy-five thousand dollars that we have to come up with to make this happen is a humbling hurdle to ponder. He hopes to start these procedures next year. In the mean time we continue to carefully choreograph each day in our personal dance of intimacy. There may be more depression, physical pain, and new places that our relationship will take us. I think it's cliché and altogether bullshit to believe "love endures all things." Sometimes love does *not* endure. However, when it does, it changes...it has to change.

Our love doesn't look the same as it did when we began this journey three and a half years ago (feels more like a *decade* at this point!). Our love has lost some things. It has gained others. My love for Rhys has transformed, as his body has done the same. At times one has set the precedent for the other, and at other times the roles have changed. What has remained a constant for me is the intangible answer to the question, "Who is Rhys?" The spirit, his essence, or whatever label you put on the elusive energy that animates our bodies, is the part of Rhys that I am most in love with. I want to be near that energy no matter what body it inhabits. Is it so different from those who have had their lover greatly changed from an accident or an illness? Does the love diminish with the physical changes? How shallow would we be if this were the true gauge of our attraction to the people we love?

All of us have absolute ownership of only one thing in this life: our bodies. And all of us have the physicality and limitations of our individual selves. Each day I wake up with the hearing loss in my right ear. My deafness is a hidden disability, born of years of experience at positioning myself to the right of anyone speaking. I stand naked every day before the mirror, and gaze at the jagged reflection of the scar that runs down eight inches of my belly. The cancer is only a memory, yet the scar is a permanent reminder of all that has changed in me. My body is becoming a physical memoir, the stories of my life are written all over it. The same is true for all of us. To this length, I venture to say that through Rhys' transition I have learned that change is just that: change. Neither good nor bad. It all lies in perception. Rhys has changed and my response to his newness has been to make changes in myself. Our love has not only survived but it has grown…immensely. I believe that my focus on the intangible nature of the whole gender idea leaves a space for the constant gender fluidity of not only Rhys, but of myself as well. I have found peace when I am confronted with the occasional curiosity of others. "What does that make *you*?" is no longer a question that sends me into a place of anger and self-doubt. The answer is it doesn't *make* me anything. I love Rhys, and that is all the response needed.

I can't help myself but to project into the future. I wonder if a day will come when the knowledge of Rhys being born in a female body will become a distant, infrequent memory. Against his wishes I have kept many photos of our life together prior to his transition. I still like (or need) to look at *her*. I can't help myself. *She* will always be who *he* was when I fell in love with *her/him*. Perhaps ten years from now I will feel the same indifference he does now about those pictures. I highly doubt it, but perhaps. I try to remember to be gentle with myself about holding on to this small piece from where we came.

Recently I read a book by the author Eckhart Tolle. In it he states his belief that the only thing that truly exists is this very moment. The future has not happened yet, and the past is now only memory. It makes me sad to think about that last part in relationship to Rhys, but this thought has now become a mantra of sorts for me.

I can deal with *this* moment.

When I get too far into my thoughts about what has changed between us and how much more may change in the future, I am overcome with anxiety and fear. So I try and stick with *this* moment. Right now this is what I know:

Rhys is sitting in his chair across from me, reading with the cat in his lap.

We are both in perfect health.

Our house is warm against the November cold.

My children are safe and happy.

We have a few *really* good friends.

I love Rhys.

Rhys loves me.

A lot has changed, and a lot more will, but right now all of us are who we are in this very moment, and none other. When I think of it that way gender seems a trivial detail, and that's what I would prefer it to be. I am a human being, and what makes me unique is not the work I do, the people I love, or the gender I present. My uniqueness lies in that intangible place within. Call it soul, personality or whatever, but it can't be defined by any one characteristic. This is how I love Rhys and will continue to love him...one transforming moment at a time.

34770253R00114